9th Workshop on Asian Language Resources 2011

Held at the 5th International Joint Conference on Natural Language Processing 2011 (IJCNLP 2011)

Chiang Mai, Thailand
12-13 November 2011

ISBN: 978-1-62276-455-6

Printed from e-media with permission by:

Curran Associates, Inc.
57 Morehouse Lane
Red Hook, NY 12571

Some format issues inherent in the e-media version may also appear in this print version.

Printed by Curran Associates, Inc. (2012)

Association for Computational Linguistics
209 N. Eighth Street
Stroudsburg, Pennsylvania 18360

Phone: 1-570-476-8006
Fax: 1-570-476-0860

acl@aclweb.org

Additional copies of this publication are available from:

Curran Associates, Inc.
57 Morehouse Lane
Red Hook, NY 12571 USA
Phone: 845-758-0400
Fax: 845-758-2634
Email: curran@proceedings.com
Web: www.proceedings.com

Table of Contents

Preface

We are happy to publish this volume that contains the papers presented at the 9th Workshop on Asian Language Resources hosted by the Asian Federation of Natural Language Processing, held in conjunction with the International Joint Conference on Natural Language Processing (IJCNLP 2011) in November 12-13, 2011 in Chiang Mai. The workshop and, needless to say, this volume intend to highlight the continually increasing as well as diversified efforts in Asia to build multilingual and multi-modal language resources and their applications through the use of ICTs. Corollary to these thriving endeavors, there is also a need for international standards within the region. Thus, the workshop on its second day is held in cooperation with ISO/TC37/SC4, which develops international standards for language resources management.

All papers submitted for presentation went through a double blind-review process and were evaluated by two or three members of the program committee. Twelve of the submitted papers (or 71 percent) were chosen for presentation at the conference, which are published in this volume. We want to thank all those who submitted papers for review and those who provided manuscripts for publication in these proceedings. We also want to give special thanks to the effort and hard work of our reviewers, whose commitment reflects their dedication to the growth of NLP in the region.

Rachel Edita O. Roxas (Chair)
Sarmad Hussain (Co-Chair)
Key-Sun Choi (Co-Chair)

Organizers:

Asian Language Resource Committee (ALRC)
Asian Federation of NLP (AFNLP, www.afnlp.org)

Co-Organizers:

ISO/TC37/SC4
East Asian Forum on Terminology (EAFTERM)

Program Committee:

Rachel Edita O. Roxas (Chair) - De La Salle University, Philippines
Sarmad Hussain (Co-Chair) - CLE-KICS, UET Lahore, Pakistan
Key-Sun Choi (Co-Chair) - Dept. of CS, KAIST, Korea

Mirna Adriani - University of Indonesia, Indonesia
Pushpak Bhattacharyya - IIT-Bombay, India
Miriam Butt - University of Konstanz, Germany
Thatsanee Charoenporn - NECTEC, Thailand
Rowena Cristina Guevara - University of the Philippines Diliman, Philippines
Hitoshi Isahara - NICT, Japan
Emi Izumi - NICT, Japan
Chu-Ren Huang - Hong Kong Polytechnic University, and Academia Sinica, Taiwan
Zhang Huarui - Peking University, China
Haizhou Li - I2R, Singapore
Chi Mai Luong - IOIT, Vietnamese Academy of Science and Technology, Vietnam
Ruli Marunung - University of Indonesia, Indonesia
Yoshiki Mikami - Nagaoka University of Technology, Japan
Sakrange Turance Nandasara - University of Colombo, School of Computing, Sri Lanka
Hammam Riza - IPTEKnet-BPPT, Indonesia
Kiyoaki Shirai - JAIST, Japan
Virach Sornlertlamvanich - NECTEC, Thailand
Takenobu Tokunaga - Tokyo Institute of Technology, Japan
Ruvan Weerasinghe - University of Colombo, School of Computing, Sri Lanka
Chai Wutiwiwatchai - NECTEC, Thailand
Yogendra Yadava - Tribhuvan University, Nepal

We wish to thank our sponsors

Gold Sponsors

www.google.com

www.baidu.com

The Office of Naval Research (ONR)

The Asian Office of Aerospace Research and Development (AOARD)

Department of Systems Engineering and Engineering Managment, The Chinese University of Hong Kong

Silver Sponsors

Microsoft Corporation

Bronze Sponsors

Chinese and Oriental Languages Information Processing Society (COLIPS)

Supporter

Thailand Convention and Exhibition Bureau (TCEB)

We wish to thank our sponsors

Organizers

Asian Federation of Natural Language Processing (AFNLP)

National Electronics and Computer Technology Center (NECTEC), Thailand

Sirindhorn International Institute of Technology (SIIT), Thailand

Rajamangala University of Technology Lanna (RMUTL), Thailand

Maejo University, Thailand

Chiang Mai University (CMU), Thailand

Conference Program

Saturday, November 12, 2011

9:00–10:00 *Participation in Language Resource Development and Sharing (Invited Talk)*
Virach Sornlertlamvanich

Session Chair: Rachel Edita Roxas

10:00–10:30 Coffee/Tea Break

Session 1: Language Resources

Session Chair: Allan Borra

10:30–10:50 *Towards a Computational Semantic Analyzer for Urdu*
Annette Hautli and Miriam Butt

10:50–11:10 *Engineering a Deep HPSG for Mandarin Chinese (Short Paper)*
Yi Zhang, Rui Wang and Yu Chen

11:10–11:30 *Experiences in Building Urdu WordNet*
Farah Adeeba and Sarmad Hussain

11:30–11:50 *Bantay-Wika: towards a better understanding of the dynamics of Filipino culture and linguistic change (Short Paper)*
Joel Ilao, Rowena Cristina Guevara, Virgilio Llenaresas, Eilene Antoinette Narvaez and Jovy Peregrino

11:50–12:00 Panel Discussion

12:00–14:00 Lunch

Saturday, November 12, 2011 (continued)

Session 2: Corpus

Session Chair: Stephen Beale

14:00–14:20 *Error Detection for Treebank Validation*
Bharat Ram Ambati, Rahul Agarwal, Mridul Gupta, Samar Husain and Dipti Misra Sharma

14:20–14:40 *Multi-stage Annotation using Pattern-based and Statistical-based Techniques for Automatic Thai Annotated Corpus Construction*
Nattapong Tongtep and Thanaruk Theeramunkong

14:40–15:00 *Feasibility of Leveraging Crowd Sourcing for the Creation of a Large Scale Annotated Resource for Hindi English Code Switched Data: A Pilot Annotation*
Mona Diab and Ankit Kamboj

15:00–15:20 *Philippine Languages Online Corpora: Status, issues, and prospects*
Shirley Dita and Rachel Edita Roxas

15:20–15:30 Panel Discussion

15:30–16:00 Coffee/Tea Break

Session 3: NLP Tools

Session Chair: Mona Diab

16:00–16:20 *Word Disambiguation in Shahmukhi to Gurmukhi Transliteration*
Tejinder Singh Saini and Gurpreet Singh Lehal

16:20–16:40 *A Grammar Checker for Tagalog using LanguageTool*
Nathaniel Oco and Allan Borra

16:40–17:00 *Linguist's Assistant: A Resource For Linguists*
Stephen Beale and Tod Allman

17:00–17:20 *Providing Ad Links to Travel Blog Entries Based on Link Types*
Aya Ishino, Hidetsugu Nanba and Toshiyuki Takezawa

Saturday, November 12, 2011 (continued)

17:20–17:30 Panel Discussion

Sunday, November 13, 2011

10:30–12:00 *Discourse Structures (SemAF-DS)*
Koiti Hasida

12:00–14:00 Lunch

14:00–15:30 *Tool Interchange Formats*
Nancy Ide

15:30–16:00 Coffee/Tea Break

16:00–16:30 *WG Plenary*
Nancy Ide and Kiyong Lee

Participation in Language Resource Development and Sharing

Virach Sornlertlamvanich
National Electronics and Computer Technology Center
Pathumthani, Thailand
virach.sornlertlamvanich@nectec.or.th

Abstract

Language resources are really much required for understanding and modeling the language in the present approaches. The language that has a rich language resource gains a big benefit in making a big advance in language processing. On the other hand, the less resource language is struggling with preparing a large enough language resource such as raw text or annotated corpora. It is a labor intensive and time consuming task. Moreover, computerization of the text is another non-trivial effort. There needs a supportive computing environment in inputting, encoding, retrieving, analysis, etc.. Learning from the rich resource languages, we gradually collecting the resource and preparing the necessary tools. Through many efforts in the recent years, we can see some significant outcomes from PAN localization project (2004-2007, 2007-2101, http://www.panl10n.net/), ADD (2006-2010, http://www.tcllab.org/), Asian WordNet (http://asianwordnet.org/), Hindi WordNet (http://www.cfilt.iitb.ac.in/wordnet/webhwn/), BEST (since 2009, Thai Word Segmentation Software Contest, http://thailang.nectec.or.th/best/) and many NLP summer schools. The activities gain a big potential in leveraging the NLP tools development and research personnel development. It results in a big growth of Asian language resource development and research. With the spirit of sharing on social networking, the resources can efficiently be developed to a satisfied amount in a reasonable time scale. Asian WordNet is an example of developing a set of 13 languages of Wordnet connected via Princeton WordNet. Thai WordNet is open for online collaborative development. About 70K synsets and 80K words of Thai WordNet are available online. Thai-Lao conversion is an approach to exhibit the advantage in utilization of language similarity to increase the other language resource. Lao WordNet is created by converting from Thai WordNet by using the phoneme transfer approach. Taking the advantage of language similarity, the language corpus can be obtained by a quick conversion rule. In this case, the study of direct transfer is much more efficient than creating from the scratch. Currently, most of the above mentioned results are open to public for at least research purpose. However, more and more language resources are still needed to improve the language processing. The possible of online collaborative development and sharing is a key factor in the language resource development.

Proceedings of the 9th Workshop on Asian Language Resources, page 1,
Chiang Mai, Thailand, November 12 and 13, 2011.

A Grammar Checker for Tagalog using LanguageTool

Nathaniel Oco
Center for Language Technologies
College of Computer Studies
De La Salle University
2401 Taft Avenue
Malate, Manila City
1004 Metro Manila
Philippines
nathanoco@yahoo.com

Allan Borra
Center for Language Technologies
College of Computer Studies
De La Salle University
2401 Taft Avenue
Malate, Manila City
1004 Metro Manila
Philippines
borgz.borra@delasalle.ph

Abstract

This document outlines the use of Language Tool for a Tagalog Grammar Checker. Language Tool is an open-source rule-based engine that offers grammar and style checking functionalities. The details of the various linguistic resource requirements of Language Tool for the Tagalog language are outlined and discussed. These are the tagger dictionary and the rule file that use the notation of Language Tool. The expressive power of Language Tool's notation is analyzed and checked if Tagalog linguistic phenomena are captured or not. The system was tested using a collection of sentences and these are the results: 91% precision rate, 51% recall rate, 83% accuracy rate.

1 Credits

LanguageTool was developed by Naber (2003). It can run as a stand-alone program and as an extension for OpenOffice.Org[1] and LibreOffice[2]. LanguageTool is distributed through Language-Tool's website: http://www.languagetool.org/.

2 Introduction

LanguageTool is an open-source style and grammar checker that follows a manual-based rule-creation approach.

LanguageTool utilizes rules stored in an xml file to analyze and check text input. The text input is separated into sentences, each sentence is separated into words, and each word is assigned a part-of-speech tag based on the declarations in the Tagger Dictionary. The words and their part-of-speech are used to check for patterns that match those declared in the rule file. If there is a pattern match, an error message is shown to the user. Currently, LanguageTool supports Belarusian, Catalan, Danish, Dutch, English, Esperanto, French, Galician, Icelandic, Italian, Lithuanian, Malayalam, Polish, Romanian, Russian, Slovak, Slovenian, Spanish, Swedish, and Ukrainian to a certain degree.

Tagalog is the basis for the Filipino language, the official language of the Philippines. According to a data collected by Cheng et al. (2009), there are 22,000,000 native speakers of Tagalog. This makes it the highest in the country, followed by Cebuano with 20,000,000 native speakers. Tagalog is very rich in morphology, Ramos (1971) stated that Tagalog words are normally composed of root words and affixes. Dimalen and Dimalen (2007) described Tagalog as a language with "high degree of inflection".

Jasa et al. (2007) stated that the number of available Tagalog grammar checkers is limited. Tagalog is a very rich language and Language-Tool is a flexible language. The development of Tagalog support for LanguageTool provides a readily-available Tagalog grammar checker that can be easily updated.

3 Related Works

Ang et al. (2002) developed a semantic analyzer that has the capability to check semantic relationships in a Tagalog sentence. Jasa et al. (2007) and Dimalen and Dimalen (2007) both developed syntax-based Filipino grammar checker extensions for OpenOffice.Org Writer. In syntax-based grammar checkers, error-checking is based on the parser. An input is considered correct if

1 OpenOffice.Org is available at http://www.openoffice.org/
2 LibreOffice is available at http://www.libreoffice.org/

Proceedings of the 9th Workshop on Asian Language Resources, pages 2–9,
Chiang Mai, Thailand, November 12 and 13, 2011.

parsing succeeds, erroneous if parsing fails. Naber (2003) explained that syntax-based grammar checkers need a complete grammar to function. Erroneous sentences that are not covered by the grammar can be flagged as error-free input.

4 LanguageTool Resources

Discussed here are the different language resources required by the tool. The notations, formats, and acquisition of resources are outlined and discussed.

4.1 Tagger Dictionary

Language Tool utilizes a dictionary file, called the Tagger Dictionary. The tagger dictionary, which contains word declarations, is utilized in pattern matching to identify and tag words with their part-of-speech.

The tagger dictionary can be a txt file, a dict file, or an FSA-encoded[3] dict file. The tagger dictionary contains three columns, separated by a tag. The first column is the inflected form. The second column is the base form. The third column is the part-of-speech tag. The format for the Tagalog tagger dictionary follows the three-column format. The first column is the inflected form, which could contain ligatures. The second column is similar to the first column, except that ligatures were omitted. This serves as the base form. The third column is the proposed tag, which is composed of the part-of-speech or POS of the word and the corresponding attribute-value pair, separated by a white space character. This serves as the POS tag. Figure 1 shows a sample declaration from the Tagalog tagger dictionary.

```
doktor  doktor  NCOM
ako     ako     PANP ST S
kumakain        kumakain        VACF IN
nasa    nasa    PRLO
mga     mga     DECP
hoy     hoy     INTR
```

Figure 1. Tagalog Tagger Dictionary Example Declarations

Evaluation and test data from different researches on Tagalog POS Tagging (Bonus, 2004; Cheng and Rabo, 2006; Miguel and Roxas, 2007) were used to come up with almost 8,000 word declarations for the Tagalog Tagger Dictionary.

4.2 Tagset for the Tagger Dictionary

A tagset for the Tagalog tagger dictionary is proposed. The tagset is based on the tagset developed by Rabo and Cheng (2006) and the modifications by Miguel and Roxas (2007). The discussions on Tagalog affixation (1971) and case system of Tagalog verbs (1973) by Ramos, verb aspect and verb focus by Cena and Ramos (1990), different Tagalog part-of-speech by Cubar and Cubar (1994), and inventory of verbal affixes by Otanes and Schachter (1972) were taken into account.

Table 1 shows the proposed noun tags. Nouns were classified into proper nouns, common nouns, and abbreviations. Kroeger (1993) explained that the determiners used for proper nouns and common nouns are different to a certain degree.

NOUN: [tag] [semantic class]	
Tag	
NPRO	Proper Noun
NCOM	Common Noun
NABB	Abbreviation

Table 1. Noun Tags

Table 2 shows the proposed pronoun tags. Grammatical person and plurality attribute were added to aid in distinguishing different types of pronouns.

PRONOUN: [tag] [grammatical person] [plurality]	
Tag	
PANP	"ang" Pronouns
PNGP	"ng" Pronouns
PSAP	"sa" Pronouns
PAND	"ang" Demonstratives
PNGD	"ng" Demonstratives
PSAD	"sa" Demonstratives
PFOP	Found Pronouns
PINP	Interrogative Pronouns
PCOP	Comparison Pronouns
PIDP	Indefinite Pronouns
POTH	Other
Grammatical Person	
ST	1st person
ND	2nd person
RD	3rd person
NU	Null

[3] FSA stands for Finite State Automata. Morfologik was used to build the binary automata. Morfologik is available at http://sourceforge.net/projects/morfologik/files/morfologik-stemming/

Plurality	
S	Singular
P	Plural
B	Both

Table 2. Pronoun Tags

Table 3 shows the proposed verb tags. Verb focus and verb aspect were added. The verb focus can indicate the thematic role the subject is taking. This is useful for future works.

VERB: [focus] [aspect]	
Focus	
VACF	Actor Focus
VOBF	Object / Goal Focus
VBEF	Benefactive Focus
VLOF	Locative Focus
VINF	Instrument Focus
VOTF	Other
Aspect	
NE	Neutral
CM	Completed
IN	Incompleted
CN	Contemplated
RC	Recently Completed
OT	Other

Table 3. Verb Tags

Table 4 shows the proposed adjective tags. Plurality was added to handle number agreement. Kroeger (1993) stated that if the plurality of the nominative argument does not match the plurality of the adjective or the predicate, the sentence considered ungrammatical.

ADJECTIVE: [tag] [plurality]	
Tag	
ADMO	Modifier
ADCO	Comparative
ADSU	Superlative
ADNU	Numeral
ADUN	Unaffixated
ADOT	Other
Plurality	
S	Singular
P	Plural
N	Null

Table 4. Adjective Tags

Table 5 shows the proposed adverb tags. An additional attribute was added to distinguish the POS of the word being modified. Ramos (1971) stated that adverbs in Tagalog can modify verbs, adjectives, and other adverbs.

ADVERB: [tag] [modifies]	
Tag	
AVMA	Manner
AVNU	Numeral
AVDE	Definite
AVEO	Comparison, group I
AVET	Comparison, group II
AVCO	Comparative, group I
AVCT	Comparative, group II
AVSO	Superlative, group I
AVST	Superlative, group II
AVSC	Slight comparison
AVAY	Agree (Panang-ayon)
AVGI	Disagree (Pananggi)
AVAG	Possibility (Pang-agam)
AVPA	Frequency (Pamanahon)
AVOT	Other
Modifies	
VE	Verb
AD	Adjective
AV	Adverb
AL	Applicable to All

Table 5. Adverb Tags

Conjunctions, prepositions, determiners, interjections, ligatures, particles, enclitic, punctuation, and auxiliary words are also part of the proposed tagset. These tags however, do not contain additional properties or corresponding attribute-value pairs. Overall, the tagset has a total of 87 tags from 14 POS and lexical categories.

4.3 Rule File

The rule file is an xml file used to check errors in a sentence. If a pattern declared in the rule matches the input sentence, an error is shown to the user.

The rule file, case insensitive by default, is composed of several rule categories which may cover but is not limited to spelling, grammar, style, and punctuation errors. Each rule category is composed of one or more rules or rule groups. Each rule is composed of different elements and attributes. The three basic elements a rule has are pattern, message, and example. The pattern element is where the error to be matched is declared. The message element is where the feedback and suggestion, if applicable, is declared. The example element is where incorrect and correct examples are declared. Figure 2 shows a pseudocode that describes what happens in the event a pattern is matched and Figure 3 shows an example rule in the Tagalog rule file.

```
if(pattern in rule file = pattern in input) {
        mark error;
        show feedback;
        provide suggestions if applicable;
}
```

Figure 2. Pseudocode

```
<rule id="MGA_MGA" name="mga mga
(ang mga)">
        <pattern case_sensitive="no"
        mark_from="0">
                <token>mga</token>
                <token>mga</token>
        </pattern>
        <message>Do you mean
                <suggestion>ang
                \2</suggestion>? "mga" can
                not be followed by another
                "mga".
        </message>
        <short>Word Repetition</short>
        <example correction="ang mga"
        type="incorrect">Maganda
        <marker>mga mga</marker>
        tanawin.</example>
        <example type="correct">Maganda
        <marker>ang mga</marker>
        tanawin.</example>
</rule>
```

Figure 3. Rule File Declaration for “ang ang” word repetition

Pattern matching can utilize tokens, POS tags, and a combination of both to properly capture errors. Regular expressions [4] are also used to simplify or merge several rules. Figure 4 shows different examples of using regular expression. Different methods of pattern-matching explained in LanguageTool’s website are shown in Figure 5. It should be noted that if a particular error is not covered by the tagger dictionary and the rule file, the error will not be detected.

[4] Standard Regular Expression Engine of Java. Described at: http://download.oracle.com/javase/1,5.0/docs/api/java/util/regex/Pattern.html

```
ding? = din or ding
ring? = rin or ring
.*[aeiou] = any word that ends in a vowel
.*[bcdfghjklmnpqrstvwxyz] = any word that
ends in a consonant
```

Figure 4. Regular expression usage

```
<token bla="x">think</token>
matches the word “think”

<token regexp="yes">think|say</token>
matches the regular expression think|say, i.e.
the word “think” or “say”

<token postag="VB" />
<token>house</token>
matches a base form verb followed by the
word house.

<token>cause</token> <token regexp="yes"
negate="yes">and|to</token>
matches the word “cause” followed by any
word that is not “and” or “to”

<token postag="SENT_START" /> <to-
ken>foobar</token>
matches the word “foobar” only at the begin-
ning of a sentence
```

Figure 5. Different methods of pattern-matching described in LangaugeTool’s website

The following resources were used as basis in developing rules: Makabagong Balarila ng Pilipino (Ramos, 1971), Writing Filipino Gramamar: Traditions and Trends (Cubar and Cubar, 1994), Modern Tagalog: Grammatical Explanations and Exercises for Non-native Speakers (Cena and Ramos, 1990), Tagalog Reference Grammar (Otanes and Schachter, 1972) and Phrase Structure and Grammatical Relations in Tagalog (Kroeger, 1993).

5 Tagalog Grammar Checking

Errors are classified into three types: wrong word, missing word, and transposition of words. This section discusses the different types of errors and the corresponding method for capturing these errors. Figure 6 shows a pseudocode explaining how an error is classified.

```
if(POS sequence != unoccurring)
        Wrong Word;
else if(POS sequence = unoccurring)
        if(POS sequence before !=
        unoccurring || POS after != unoccur-
        ring)
                Missing Word;
        else
                Transposition;
```

Figure 6. Pseudocode

5.1 Wrong Words

Wrong words are often caused by using the wrong determiner and affixation rule. Also, morphophonemic change and verb focus are often not taken into consideration. There are cases where relying on part-of-speech alone will not capture certain errors. To address this issue, grammatical person and plurality of pronouns, focus and aspect of verbs, plurality of adjectives, and word modified by adverbs were considered in developing the tagset. Consider the example in Figure 7. Both have the same POS but only one is correct. Kroeger (1993) pointed out that plurality in adjectives is demonstrated by the reduplication of the first syllable. An error caused by the disagreement of the plurality of the adjective and the plurality of the nominative argument can not be handled by considering the part-of-speech only.

Correct:	
Magaganda	*kami.*
Adjective	1st person Pronoun
Plural	Plural
Beautiful	we.
We are beautiful.	
Incorrect:	
Magaganda	*ako.*
Adjective	1st person Pronoun
Plural	Singular
Beaautiful	me.
(For: I am beautiful)	

Figure 7. Number Agreement

Consider the sentences in Figure 8. The enclitic "*din*" is used if the last letter of the preceding word is a consonant. Otherwise, "*rin*" is used. Cena and Ramos (1990) explained that sound and letter changes occur in affixation and even in word boundaries. "*din*" and "*rin*" is one of many examples. To address this, a simple token matching is performed. Regular expressions were employed to make rule files shorter.

> Correct:
> *Magnanakaw din siya.*
> He is also thief.
>
> Incorrect:
> *Magnanakaw rin siya.*
> (For: He is also thief.)

Figure 8. Sound and Letter Change

Other errors like proper adverb and ligature usage also fall into this type of error.

5.2 Missing Words

Missing words are often due to missing determiners, particles, markers, and other words composed of several letters. Usually, missing words cause irregular and unoccurring POS sequence. Figure 9 illustrates an example. Unoccurring POS sequence are checked and matched against specific rules. The missing word is added to the sentence as feedback. In the sentences in Figure 9, it is unnatural for a pronoun to be immediately followed by an adjective. Missing words are captured by looking for unoccurring POS sequence often caused by a missing word.

Correct:		
Ikaw	*ay*	*maganda.*
Pronoun	Marker	Adjective
You		beautiful
You are beautiful.		
Incorrect:		
Ikaw	*maganda.*	
Pronoun	Adjective	
You	beautiful	
(For: You are beautiful)		

Figure 9. Missing Lexical Marker "*ay*"

5.3 Transposition

The process of detecting errors caused by transposition is similar to missing words. The main difference is tokens and POS tags before and after the unoccurring POS sequence are considered and checked for any irregularities.

6 Performance of Language Tool: Results and Analysis

The system was initially tested using a collection of sentences. The collection is composed of evaluation data used in FiSSAn (Ang et al., 2002), LEFT (Chan et al., 2006), and PanPam (Jasa et al., 2007). Test data used by Dimalen (2003) examples from books (Kroeger, 1993; Ramos, 1971), and additional test data are also part of the collection. A total of 272 sentences from the collection were used. Table 6 shows a summary of figures. 186 out of 190 error-free sentences were marked as error-free, 4 out of 190 error-free sentences were marked as erroneous, 42 out of 82 erroneous sentences were marked as erroneous, and 40 out of 82 erroneous sentences were marked as error-free.

Sentences	Correctly Flagged	Incorrectly Flagged	Total
Error-free	186	4	190
Erroneous	42	40	82
Total	228	44	272

Table 6. Summary of Figures

The test showed that the system has a 91% precision rate, 51% recall rate, and 83% accuracy rate. Figure 10, Figure 11, and Figure 12 show the formulas used for precision, recall, and accuracy, respectively. True Positives refer to erroneous evaluation data properly flagged by the system as erroneous. False Positives refer to error-free evaluation data flagged by the system as erroneous. True Negatives refer to error-free evaluation data properly flagged by the system as error-free. False Negatives refer to erroneous evaluation data flagged by the system as error-free.

$$\frac{TruePositives}{TruePositives + FalsePositives}$$

Figure 10. Precision Formula

$$\frac{TruePositives}{TruePositives + FalseNegatives}$$

Figure 11. Recall Formula

$$\frac{TruePositives + TrueNegatives}{TotalNumberOfEvaluationData}$$

Figure 12. Accuracy Formula

The system flagged 4 error-free sentences as erroneous. This is mainly because of wrong declarations in the tagger dictionary file. Figure 13 shows one of the sentences. In the tagger dictionary, "*mag-aral*" was declared as a noun and "*maingay*" was declared both as an adverb and as an adjective. In the Tagalog language, if a common noun is preceded by an adjective, there should be a ligature between them. Figure 14 demonstrates proper Tagalog ligature usage.

Umalis	*ang*	*mabait*
Verb	Det	Adjective
Leave	the	good
ngunit	*maingay*	*mag-aral.*
Conjunct	Adverb	Verb
but	noisy	study

Figure 13. Flagged as erroneous

Root word ends with a vowel, add "-ng"

Matalino	+	*bata*
Adjective		Common Noun
Intelligent		Child

=*Matalinong bata*
Intelligent Child

Root word ends with the letter "n", add "-g"

Matulin	+	*bata*
Adjective		Common Noun
Fast		Child

=*Matuling bata*
Fast Child

Root word ends with a consonant, add "na"

Matapang	+	*bata*
Adjective		Common Noun
Brave		Child

=*Matapang na bata*
Brave Child

Figure 14. Ligature usage

The presence of ellipsis in one of the sentences is another reason why error-free sentences were flagged as erroneous. Ellipsis was not declared in the rule file. This resulted in two sentences being recognized as one.

The system flagged 40 out of 42 erroneous sentences as error-free. A close analysis on there errors reveal that majority of the sentences contains free-word order errors, transposition of more than 2 words, extra words. Some sentences contain errors that focus on semantic checking. Figure 15 shows 9 of these sentences. These are the type of errors that are not handled by the system and are not declared in the rule file. Future research works can focus on these areas.

Humihinga ang bangkay.
The corpse is breathing.

Nagluto ang sanggol.
The baby cooked.

Naglakad ang ahas.
The snake walked.

Kumain ang plato.
The plate ate.

Nabasag ang basong mabilis.
The fast glass shattered.

Kumain ang plato sa baso.
The plate ate at the glass.

Kumain ang aso ng plato.
The dog ate the plate.

Tumakbo ang sapatos.
The shoe ran.

Nagluto ang pusa ng pagkain.
The cat cooked food.

Figure 15. Flagged as error-free

Among the 42 erroneous sentences it correctly flagged as erroneous, the system provided the correct feedback for 41 sentences. The sentence with incorrect feedback is shown in Figure 16. The sentence, used to test free-word order, contains transposition of several words. The system detected it as a missing last word error because the determiner "*ang*" can not be the last word of a sentence.

Pinalo tatay ng makulit batang ang.

Correct Form:
Pinalo ng tatay ang batang makulit.
The father spanked the naughty child.

Figure 16. Sentence with incorrect feedback

For comparative evaluation, the same collection was tested on PanPam (Jasa et al., 2007) and these are the results: 23% precision rate, 46% recall rate, and 38% accuracy rate. Table 7 shows a summary of figures.

Sentences	Correctly Flagged	Incorrectly Flagged	Total
Error-free	68	122	190
Erroneous	38	44	82
Total	106	166	272

Table 7. PanPam Results

The comparative evaluation shows that the system scored 68% higher than PanPam in terms of precision, 5% higher in terms of recall, and 37% higher in terms of accuracy.

Overall, these findings reaffirm earlier analysis by Konchady (2009) that rule-based grammar checkers that follow a manual-based rule-creation approach tend to produce low recall rate but precision rate is above average. This is because the total number of rules isn't sufficient to cover a variety of errors. Also, because of pattern-matching, majority of the errors detected are indeed errors. It is also important to note, especially in the case of LanguageTool, that the patterns being captured are erroneous sentences and not error-free sentences. This makes rule-based grammar checkers dependent on the rules declared for error checking coverage.

LanguageTool can support the Tagalog language to a certain degree. Although developing a tagger dictionary and a rule file is a tedious task, it is necessary to create a tagger dictionary, a tagset, and rules that can handle the different Tagalog linguistic Penomena.

Acknowledgements

The authors acknowledge developers and maintainers of LanguageTool especially Daniel Naber, Dominique Pellé, and Marcin Milkowski for being instrumental to the completion of this study and to the completion of the Tagalog support for LanguageTool. The August 07, 2011 snapshot of LanguageTool would not include Tagalog support if not for their assistance. The authors also acknowledge the opinions and thoughts shared through email by Vlamir Rabo, Manu Konchady, and Mark Johnson.

References

Charibeth K. Cheng, Nathalie Rose T. Lim, and Rachel Edita O. Roxas. 2009. Philippine Language

Resources: Trends and Directions. *Proceedings of the 7th Workshop on Asian Langauge Resource (ALR7),* Singapore.

Charibeth K. Cheng and Vlamir S. Rabo. 2006. TPOST: A Template-based Part-of-Speech Tagger for Tagalog. *Journal of Research in Science, Computing, and Engineering,* Volume 3, Number 1.

Dalos D. Miguel and Rachel Edita O. Roxas. 2007. Comparative Analysis of Tagalog Part of Speech (POS) Taggers. *Proceedings of the 4th National Natural Language Processing Research Symposium (NNLPRS),* CSB Hotel, Manila. ISSN 1908-3092.

Daniel Naber. 2003. *A Rule-Based Style and Grammar Checker.* Diploma Thesis. Bielefeld University, Bielefeld.

Davis Muhajereen D. Dimalen and Editha D. Dimalen. 2007. An OpenOffice Spelling and Grammar Checker Add-in Using an Open Source External Engine as Resource Manager and Parser. *Proceedings of the 4th National Natural Language Processing Research Symposium (NNLPRS),* CSB Hotel, Manila.

Don Erick J. Bonus. 2004. A Stemming Algorithm for Tagalog Words. *Proceedings of the 4th Philippine Computing Science Congress (PSCS 2004),* University of the Philippines – Los Baños, Laguna.

Editha D. Dimalen. 2003. *A Parsing Algorithm for Constituent Structures of Tagalog.* Master's Thesis. De La Salle University, Manila.

Ernesto H. Cubar and Nelly I. Cubar. 1994. *Writing Filipino Grammar: Traditions and Trends.* New Day Publishers, Quezon City.

Erwin Andrew O. Chan, Chris Ian R. Lim, Richard Bryan S. Tan, and Marlon Cromwell N. Tong. 2006. *LEFT: Lexical Functional Grammar Based English-Filipino Translator.* Undergraduate Thesis. De La Salle University, Manila.

Fe T. Otanes and Paul Schachter. 1972. *Tagalog Reference Grammar.* University of California Press, Berkeley, CA.

LanguageTool. http://www.languagetool.org/

Manu Konchady. 2009. *Detecting Grammatical Errors in Text using a Ngram-based Ruleset.* Retrieved from: http://emustru.sourceforge.net/detecting_grammatical_errors.pdf

Michael A. Jasa, Justin O. Palisoc, and Martee M. Villa. 2007. *Panuring Pampanitikan (PanPam): A Sentence Syntax and Semantic Based Grammar Checker for Filipino.* Undergraduate Thesis. De La Salle University, Manila.

Morgan O. Ang, Sonny G. Cagalingan, Paulo Justin U. Tan, and Reagan C. Tan. 2002. *FiSSAn: Filipino Sentence Syntax and Semantic Analyzer.* Undergraduate Thesis. De La Salle University, Manila.

Paul Kroeger. 1993. *Phrase Structure and Grammartical Relations in Tagalog.* CSLI Publications, Stanford, CA.

Resty M. Cena and Teresita V. Ramos. 1990. *Modern Tagalog: Grammatical Explanations and Exercises for Non-native Speakers.* University of Hawaii Press, Honolulu, HI.

Teresita V. Ramos. 1971. *Makabagong Balarila ng Pilipino.* Rex Book Store, Manila.

Teresita V. Ramos. 1973. *The Case System of Tagalog Verbs.* Doctoral Dissertation. University of Hawaii. Honolulu, HI.

Bantay-Wika: towards a better understanding of the dynamics of Filipino culture and linguistic change

Joel P. Ilao*
Rowena Cristina L. Guevara†
Digital Signal Processing Laboratory
University of the Philippines - Diliman
Tel: +632-981-8500 local 3370
*joel.ilao@up.edu.ph
†gev@eee.upd.edu.ph

Virgilio D. Llenaresas
Eilene Antoinette G. Narvaez
Jovy M. Peregrino
Sentro ng Wikang Filipino
University of the Philippines - Diliman
Tel: +632-981-8500 local 4583
upswfdiliman@gmail.com

Abstract

The Bantay-Wika *(Language Watch)* project was started in 1994 by the University of the Philippines (UP) - Sentro ng Wikang Filipino[1] (SWF) in order to track for long periods of time how the Philippine national language is being used and how it develops, particularly in the Philippine media. The first phase of this project, from 1994 to 2004, involved the manual collection and tallying of frequency counts for all the words in eleven major Philippine tablods. With increasing online presence of Philippine news organizations, the project was revived in March 2010, with UP-SWF partnering with UP - Digital Signal Processing (DSP) laboratory. The project objectives were also re-drafted to include the development of software that would automate the process of downloading of Filipino news articles. In this paper, we further detail the goals and the history and of the Bantay-Wika project, its accomplishments and plans for future work. The project ultimately endeavors to build a computational model for language development that can guide language policy makers in a multi-lingual country such as the Philippines, in drafting policies that can effectively promote the use and development of their national language.

1 Introduction

The Philippines is an archipelago of 7,107 islands with 171 living languages spoken by 94 million inhabitants[2], thus making it the 25th most linguistically diverse nation in the world among 224 nations in the 16th edition Ethnologue (2009) (Lewis, 2009). Based on the 2000 census conducted by the National Statistics Office (NSO), there are 14 major languages[3] spoken in the country, listed next in order of decreasing number of speakers: (1) Tagalog, (2) Cebuano Bisayan, (3) Ilokano, (4) Hiligaynon Bisayan, (5) Waray (Eastern Bisayan), (6) Kapampangan, (7) Northern Bicol, (8) Chavacano, (9) Pangasinense, (10) Southern Bicol, (11) Maranao, (12) Maguindanao, (13) Kinaray-a, and (14) Tausug (Roxas et al., 2009). With such a rich Philippine linguistic profile, it is not hard to understand how difficult it must have been when in 1935, then president Manuel L. Quezon pushed for the establishment and development of language to be commonly spoken by all of the inhabitants. In the years that followed, laws have been enacted to support such cause, leading to the establishment of a national language institute tasked to identify and select the basis of the national language from the list of Philippine native languages, and to further develop the national language into a modernized and intellectualized one. Table 1 lists a brief timeline showing some milestones related to the development of the Philippine national language.

It is worth noting that the issues concerning the Philippine national language have initially been controversial and divisive, especially in the so-called language wars of the 1960's, when Senate representatives who speak the Cebuano Bisayan language challenged the selection of Tagalog language as the basis of the national language (Gonzalez, 2003). During those times until now, efforts were made to differentiate the national language from its original Tagalog base, through conscious revisions of the grammar and orthography rules

[1] 'Sentro ng Wikang Filipino' means 'Filipino Language Center'

[2] Projected population of Filipinos for 2010 according to the National Statistics Office of the Republic of the Philippines (http:www.census.gov.ph)

[3] A major language is a language spoken by at least 1 million speakers.

Proceedings of the 9th Workshop on Asian Language Resources, pages 10–17,
Chiang Mai, Thailand, November 12 and 13, 2011.

Year	Milestone Description
1935	Concept of a language commonly spoken by all inhabitants was mandated by the constitution
1936	The Tagalog language was selected as the basis of the national language
1959	The National language was named as *Pilipino* through a Department of Education order
1987	The national language was officially named as *Filipino* through the constitution

Table 1: Philippine national language development milestones.

to incorporate elements from other Philippine languages (Santos, 1940; Surian ng Wikang Pambansa [SWP], 1976; SWP, 1987; Komisyon sa Wikang Filipino [KWF], 2001; UP Sentro ng Wikang Filipino [UPSWF], 2004; UPSWF, 2008; KWF, 2009), and by renaming the national language, first as *Pilipino* in 1959, then as *Filipino* in 1987[4] in order to garb it with more sense of national appeal. Almost a quarter-century after the idea of a national language was first floated, linguists and language planners are wondering how far the Filipino language has developed and where it is headed, knowing that in a multi-lingual society such as the Philippines, it is possible that a language may retrogress and die despite sincere efforts to develop and propagate its proper use to the rest of the population (Abrams and Strogatz, 2003). In this light, effective monitoring activities of the extent and quality of actual usage of the national language by its community of users is deemed important.

2 The Bantay-Wika Project

Cognizant of the importance of the national language in fostering national unity and identity, the University of the Philippines felt it is duty-bound to actively participate in the discussions on language development. Hence, the UP - Sentro ng Wikang Filipino was created in 1990. Realizing the value of quantitatively observing the dynamics of the Filipino language usage in ascertaining the trajectory of Filipino language development, the UP-SWF started the *Bantay-Wika project* in 1994. This project initially sought to observe the rates with which new words were being introduced in the Filipino working vocabulary, as evidenced in the tabloid media. Filipino-written articles from eleven tabloids[5] with wide circulation were transcribed on a weekly basis, and a database of word frequency counts was manually built.

2.1 Tracking of competing word forms

Ferguson (1968) noted that as a language develops, it undergoes a process of standardisation by means of conventionalization of its function and use within a given language community . Guided by this language developmental framework, the Bantay-Wika project also seeks to observe how the Filipino language conventionalizes, by comparing usage rates of competing word forms. One particular class of competing word forms actually tracked in the project are borrowed words from other languages, mainly from Spanish and American English languages, owing to the influence that Spain and USA have on the Philippine society as its long-time settlers. A cursory look into Filipino-written articles would show that many of the terms used in daily news reportage which have equivalent translations in either English or Spanish manifest in any of four possible ways: (1) direct borrowing, (2) calquing or loan-translation, (3) Filipinization of spelling, and (4) use of a native word. Table 2 shows examples of each of the four ways of improvising Filipino words with foreign equivalents.

Other classes of competing word forms are spelling variants that fall under the cases listed in Table 3. Towards the end of the first phase of Bantay-Wika (year 2001 to 2004), software that can process the gathered text corpora and produce summarized reports of word counts was developed. The reports are then manually inspected to identify spelling variants. This process resulted in over 957 words tracked, of which 85 pairs were identified as spelling variants.

2.2 Philippine Culturomic Analysis based on Filipino - written news articles

The topics that a group of people write about reflect their prevailing sentiments at any given time

[4]The official name of the Philippine national language is *Filipino*.

[5]The tabloids included in the project are *Abante Tonite, Abante, Bomba, Bulgar, Imbestigador, Kabayan, People's Balita, People's Taliba, Pilipino Star Ngayon, Remate,* and *Saksi Ngayon*

Case Description	**Example**
Removal of /u/ in /uw/	kuwento / kwento
Removal of /i/ or /y/ in /iy/	superstisiyon / supertisyon Dios / Diyos
Repeating consecutive similar vowels simplified to a single vowel	saan / san mayroon / mayron
Removal of h-	hospital / ospital
Removal of prefix i-	ipinapakita / pinapakita
Simplification from /ng/ to /n/	pangsarili / pansarili
Simplification from nakapag- to naka-	nakapagsaing / nakasaing
Removal of infix -i-	maitatanggi / matatanggi
/tion/ vs. /siyon/ vs. /syon/ vs. /sion/	intervention / intervensiyon / intervensyon / interbensiyon / interbensyon
/i/ vs. /e/	galing / galeng
/o/ vs. /u/	kumpanya / kompanya
/c/ vs /k/	Cristo / Kristo
/s/ vs /z/	Luson / Luzon
/p/ vs. /f/	Pilipinas / Filipinas
/b/ vs. /v/	unibersidad / universidad
Miscellaneous cases	Maynila / Manila manyika / manika manga / mga

Table 3: Cases of Spelling Variants seen in Filipino texts

Technique	**Description**	**Example**
Direct Borrowing	verbatim use of foreign word in the sentence	shooting trophy mesa
Calquing	word-for-word translation to Filipino	tigil-putukan (*ceasefire*)
Filipinization of spelling	respelling of terms according to the Filipino alphabet	girlfrend gerlprend (*girlfriend*)
native word	use of a word found in any of the Phil. languages	bahay (*house*) mata (*eye*)

Table 2: Different ways of improvising Filipino terms with foreign equivalents

frame. Hence, it is possible to study cultural trends based on quantitative analysis of large corpora of digitized text, a field of study called Culturomics. Using normalized frequency plots of specific search words and phrases, Michel et al. (2011) were able to investigate cultural trends in fields as diverse as lexicography, the evolution of grammar, collective memory, the adoption of technology, the pursuit of fame, censorhip, and historical epidemiology. Inspired by these recent developments in Culturomics, we wanted to gain more insights into the dynamics of topics that interest Filipinos, using news corpora curated from websites of two popular Philippine tabloids. Articles were downloaded using a web-crawler from the websites of Abante[6] and Abante-tonite[7] within a two-year window period from March 22, 2009 to May 16, 2011. Each downloaded html-file was then automatically date-stamped by parsing its URL for date information, and then preprocessed by removing markup tags and scripts.

[6] http://abante.com.ph
[7] http://www.abante-tonite.com

After which, the resulting text-files were each word-tokenized and content-modified by lining up sentences one after the other. Metadata for the unannotated Abante and Abante-Tonite text corpora include URL, publication date and download date information. Table 4 describes the sizes of the Abante and Abante-tonite news text corpora. Figure 1 shows a graph of the number of downloaded articles per day for the entire observation period. Note the gaps in the dates of downloaded data for both Abante and Abante-tonite, indicating that not all dates have available downloadable data from the corresponding websites within the 2-year analysis period.

Data from Filipino-written news articles covering a 2-year analysis period from March 2009 to May 2011 was used to support the Culturomic analysis presented in this paper. *Bantay-Wika*, however, is a current project of UP-DSP and UP-SWF, with ongoing data collection efforts from Philippine news websites. The results will be published after the project has been completed. Intellectual Property rights for the text corpora are owned by the University of the Philippines - Diliman and data wil be made available to researchers for free except for requesting parties intending to use them for commercial purposes.

Feature	Abante-Tonite	Abante
No. of Downloaded Articles	31864	29713
Number of Sentences	442.1K	478.7K
Number of Unique Sentences	413.9K	397.2K
Number of Words	10.6M	10.9M
Number of Unique Words	242K	245.6K

Table 4: Description of Corpora used in Culturomic Analysis

The normalized frequency value of a given search word for a particular date was obtained by dividing the total number of sentences wherein a search word was seen at least once, with the total number of sentences obtained for the given date. Normalized frequency plots for particular search words/phrases have revealed interesting insights into the Filipino culture, as seen in the succeeding graphs. Note that the search process used for all the search words is case-insensitive.

2.2.1 Investigating the actual duration of Filipino Christmas season

The Philippines, being a predominantly Catholic Christian nation, celebrates the longest Christmas season in the world, starting from the onset of September and continuing until the feast of the Sto. Niño celebrated every third Sunday of January of the next year. Counting the number of times the words 'Christmas' and 'Pasko'[8] were mentioned in news media, whether by simple greetings or actual news reportage over a long time period can give us an idea of how intensely Filipinos celebrate Christmas. Figure 2 shows the normalized frequency plots for search words 'Christmas' and 'Pasko'. The plots show annual repeating patterns, with the initial peak found at beginning of September. The next significant peak is on the first day of December, slowly increasing to its peak on December 25, then sharply decreasing by the first week of January. Hence, it can be said that a typical Filipino's excitement over the thought of Christmas is triggered by certain events: (1) the entry of September which is the first of the '-Ber' months leading to Christmas, (2) the entry of December, the month of Christmas, and (3) the actual day of Christmas.

2.2.2 Investigating the effect of Typhoon Ondoy

On September 24, 2009, the Philippines' capital of Manila was inundated with floods when it was visited by Super Typhoon *Ondoy* (international code name: Ketsana). Images and videos of flood and devastation filled the storylines of news agencies all over the world and in various online social networking sites for many weeks. Many professed *Ondoy* to be a natural disaster that will never be erased in the collective Filipino memory. Looking at graph of normalized frequency plots for the search word 'Ondoy' of Figure 3, we see quite a different story. Approximately one month after *Ondoy* visited, news reportage has almost completely subsided. It can be seen that exactly one year later, news reporting on the topic Ondoy was only slightly revived.

[8] *Pasko* is the Filipino word for 'Christmas'

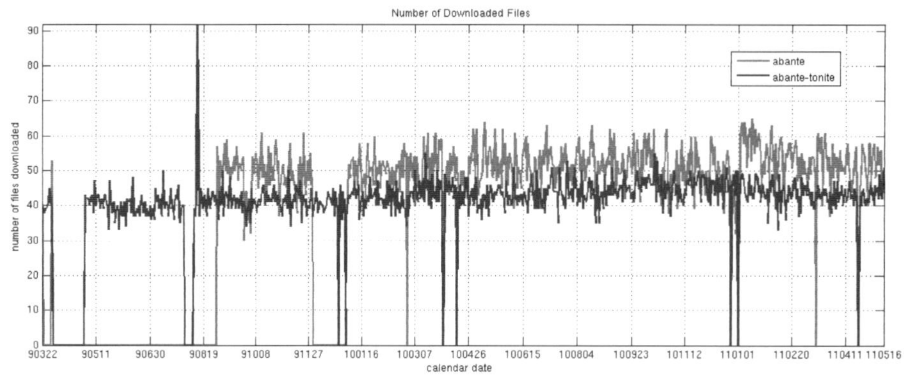

Figure 1: Distribution of downloaded files from Abante and Abante-tonite websites. *The format for the calendar date is YYMMDD where YY is the year, MM is the month, and DD is day the files were downloaded.*

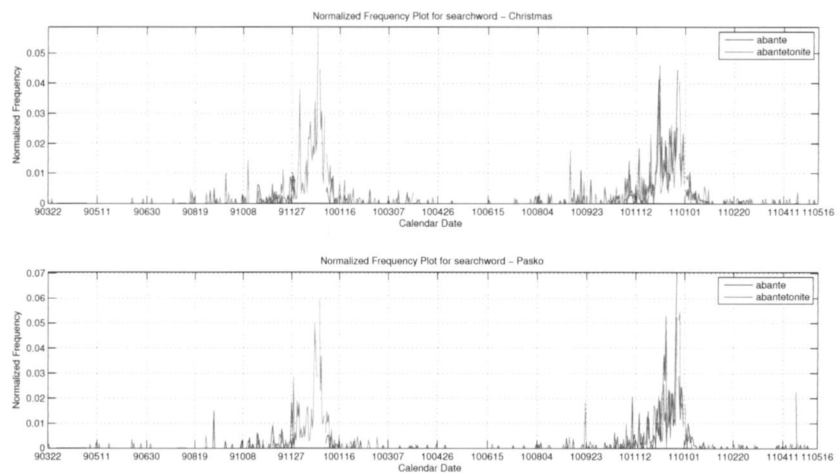

Figure 2: Frequency Plots for 'Christmas' (upper plot) and 'Pasko' (lower plot). *The format for the calendar date is YYMMDD where YY is the year, MM is the month, and DD is day the files were downloaded.*

2.2.3 Tracking the rise of popularity of the Ampatuans

Figure 4 shows the normalized frequency plots when the search word is 'Ampatuan'. Data shows that the Ampatuans were relatively under the media radar before the Nov. 23, 2009 massacre of 57 civilians and media people in Maguindanao. It was widely believed that the massacre was masterminded by the heads of the Ampatuan clan, in order to deter their political foe, Ismael Mangudadatu from running against them in the May, 2010 national elections. The next significant peak near Apr. 19, 2010 is when DOJ Acting Secretary Agra absolved the Ampatuans, resulting in an immediate public outrage. The plots clearly show that since the day of the massacre, the Ampatuans have consistently remained to be a favorite news fodder for the Philippine media.

2.2.4 Looking at an example of a linguistic fad

The normalized frequency plot of a linguistic fad such as 'Jejemon' (see Figure 5) shows a quick rise, followed by a period of relatively stable frequency plot, but ending with an abrupt fall of mentions in news and media articles. Of all the words that qualified as finalists for the Sawikaan 2010 Word of the year sponsored by the UP-SWF, only *namumutbol* did not have at least 1 entry in the Data Set. The rest of the word finalists for

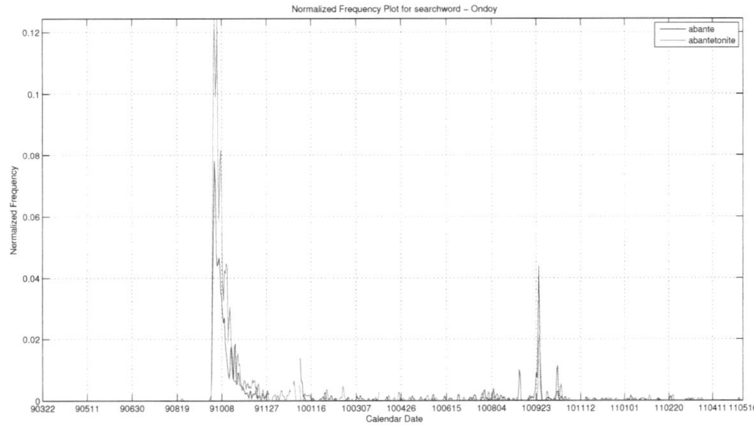

Figure 3: Frequency Plots for 'Ondoy'. *The format for the calendar date is YYMMDD where YY is the year, MM is the month, and DD is day the files were downloaded.*

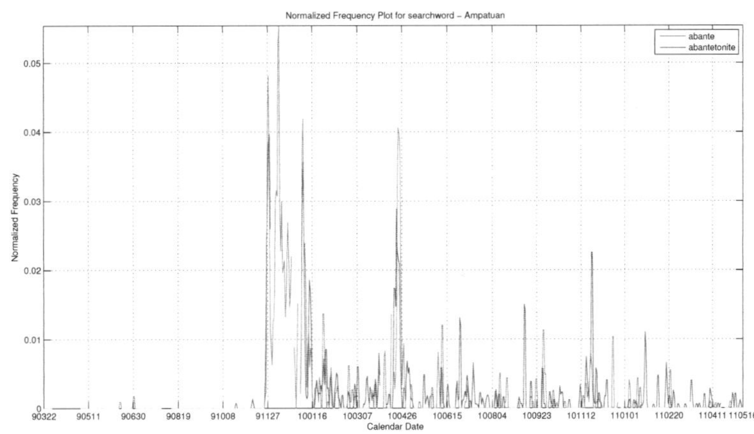

Figure 4: Frequency Plots for 'Ampatuan'. *The format for the calendar date is YYMMDD where YY is the year, MM is the month, and DD is day the files were downloaded.*

Sawikaan 2010 are *Ondoy, Ampatuan, load, Jejemon, solb, miskol, spam,* and *emo*.

2.2.5 Looking at an example of an enduring Filipino news item

Refer to Figure 6 to see the plot for the search phrase 'Cory Aquino'. Former Philippine President Cory Aquino, who was the transitory president after 26 years of Marcos dictatorship, has again been relatively popular in media news starting with rumors of her showing signs of succumbing to colon cancer early July of 2009, with reports peaking on the week of her death on August 1, 2009. Her first death anniversary shows strong public commemoration. Cory Aquino's popularity has remained consistent throughout the whole year.

3 Conclusions and Future Work

In this paper, we have described the *Bantay-Wika project*: it's goals, history, accomplishments and plans for future work. Aimed at helping language planners in attaining the goal of standardizing the use of the Philippine national language, *Bantay-Wika* is first and foremost seen as an objective and effective monitoring mechanism for tracking actual language use. Allowing the conventionalization phenomenon that characterizes the development of a language to be tracked over time enables language agencies such as the UP-SWF to test the effectiveness of their rolled out language

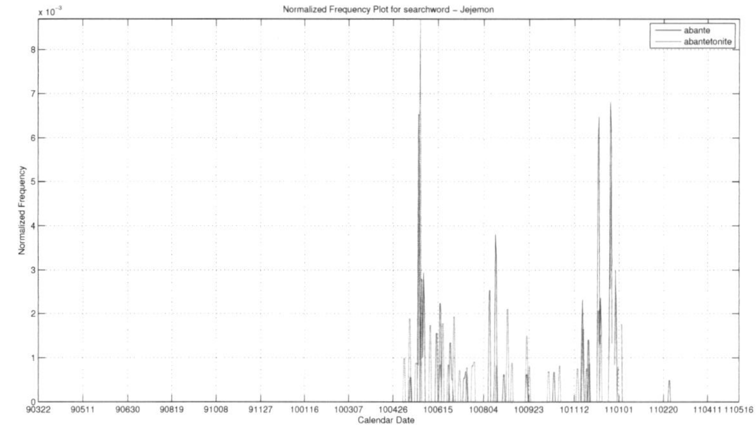

Figure 5: Frequency Plots for 'Jejemon'. *The format for the calendar date is YYMMDD where YY is the year, MM is the month, and DD is day the files were downloaded.*

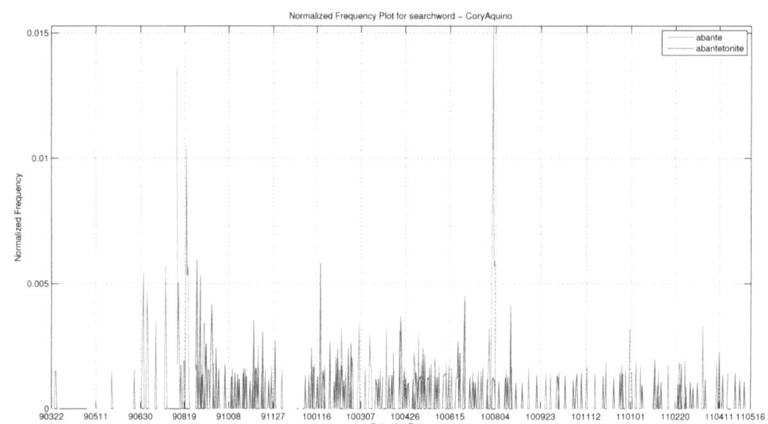

Figure 6: Frequency Plots for 'Cory Aquino'. *The format for the calendar date is YYMMDD where YY is the year, MM is the month, and DD is day the files were downloaded.*

policies and strategies, and design appropriate interventions that would aid strategies that turn out to be ineffective. In this regard, one strong motivation behind the Bantay-Wika project is to ultimately develop computational models for linguistic change, thus allowing language policy makers to reliably forecast the trajectory of language development for each language policy being implemented. Secondly, culturomic analysis of downloaded news articles covering a two-year period has provided us with more insights into the Filipino Christmas tradition, the Filipino outlook in the face of natural and man-made calamities that has attracted global attention, and linguistic fads. Observing the fluctuations in the intensity of news reportage of topics that have pervaded the Philippine national consciousness has given us an objective view of the favorite topics of Filipinos, perhaps a reflection of the values that Filipinos collectively hold dear. Efforts are currently being made to increase the coverage of the text corpora to include written work representative of each stage of the Philippine nation's colorful history starting from the 1900's to the present. With larger and more comprehensive text corpora, the authors are hopeful that more insights into how the Filipino sentiment changes with each milestone in the Philippines' history will be made apparent, thus offering a fresh look at Philippine history in a way not possible before. Finally, the data, the tools for analysis developed for this project, and the actual research findings open up different opportunities for conducting further quantitative investigative work in the areas of Philippine lexicography and diachronic linguistics, and even aid in the further understanding of Filipino philosophy. Truly, it can be said that in the case of the *Bantay-Wika project*, the use of technology has greatly expanded the reaches of scholarly inquiry.

Acknowledgments

The authors are grateful to the UP Diliman - Office of the Chancellor for funding the *Bantay-Wika project*. The first author would like to thank the Department of Science and Technology (DOST) for the Engineering Research and Development for Technology (ERDT) scholarship grant given to him.

References

Daniel M. Abrams and Steven H. Strogatz. 2003. Modeling the dynamics of language death. *Nature*, 424.

C. Ferguson. 1968. Language development. *Language Problems of Developing Nations*, pages 27–35.

Andrew B. Gonzalez. 2003. Language planning in multilingual countries: The case of the Philippines. In *Conference on Language Development, Language Revitilization and MultilingualEducation in Minority Communitites in Asia*, Bangkok, Thailand.

M. Paul Lewis. 2009. *Ethnologue: Languages of the World*. SIL International, Dallas, Texas, 16th edition.

Jean-Baptiste Michel, Yuan Kui Shen, Aviva Presser Aiden, Adrian Veres, Matthew K. Gray, The Google Books Team, Joseph P. Pickett, Dale Hoiberg, Dan Clancy, Peter Norvig, Jon Orwant, Steven Pinker, Martin A. Nowak, and Erez Lieberman Aiden. 2011. Quantitative analysis of culture using millions of digitized books. *Science*, pages 176–182.

UP Sentro ng Wikang Filipino. 2004. *Gabay sa Pagbaybay*. UP - Sentro ng Wikang Filipino.

UP Sentro ng Wikang Filipino. 2008. *Gabay sa Ispeling*. UP - Sentro ng Wikang Filipino.

Surian ng Wikang Pambansa. 1976. *Mga Tuntunin sa Ortograpiyang Fiipino*. Surian ng Wikang Pambansa.

Surian ng Wikang Pambansa. 1987. *Alpabeto at Patnubay sa Ispeling ng Wikang Filipino*. Surian ng Wikang Pambansa.

Rachel Edita Roxas, Charibeth Cheng, and Nathalie Rose Lim. 2009. Philippine language resources: trends and directions. In *7th Workshop on Asian Language Resources*, Singapore.

Komisyon sa Wikang Filipino. 2001. *Revisyon ng Alfabeto at Patnubay sa Ispeling ng Wikang Filipino*. Komisyon sa Wikang Filipino.

Komisyon sa Wikang Filipino. 2009. *Gabay sa Ortograpiyang Pilipino*. Komisyon sa Wikang Filipino.

Lope K. Santos. 1940. *Balarila ng Wikang Pambansa*. Surian ng Wikang Pambansa.

Engineering a Deep HPSG for Mandarin Chinese

Yi Zhang **Rui Wang** **Yu Chen**
LT-Lab, German Reserach Center for Artificial Intelligence, Saarbrücken, Germany
{yzhang,rwang}@coli.uni-sb.de, yuchen@dfki.de

Abstract

In this paper, we present our on-going grammar development effort towards a linguistically precise and broad coverage grammar for Mandarin Chinese in the framework of HPSG. The use of LinGO Grammar Matrix facilitates the quick start of the development. We propose a series of linguistic treatments for a list of interesting phenomena. The analyses are largely compatible with the HPSG framework. In addition, the grammar also composes semantic representations in Minimum Recursion Semantics. Preliminary tests of the grammar on a phenomenon-oriented test suite show encouraging precision and coverage.

1 Introduction

Broad coverage in-depth and accurate linguistic processing is desirable for both linguistic studies and practical NLP applications. In recent years, several competing linguistic frameworks emerge with proper expressive power and good computational properties. Typically offered by such frameworks are not only the description of the syntactic structures, but also the ways in which meanings are composed. Among the most popular frameworks are CCG, TAG, LFG and HPSG.

With the increasing availability of deep linguistic processing platforms, large-scale grammar resource development becomes possible. The past experience on large-scale grammar engineering shows that it is a long-term undertaking, which amounts to years or decades of both labor- and intelligence-intensive work. More recently, it has been shown that such process could be largely accelerated by the accumulative experience from various grammar development projects. Also, the data-driven techniques reduce the tedious repetitive work and allow grammar writers to focus on the challenging phenomena.

Encouraged by these breakthroughs, we have seen the emergence of various grammar development projects in the last decade, not only for languages with large speaker population, but also for endangered or extinct languages (Bender, 2008). Despite the huge population of Mandarin Chinese native speakers, strikingly few attempts have been made so far to formally describe the language within the above-mentioned modern linguistic frameworks. This is partially due to the fact that Mandarin Chinese is relatively less grammaticalized in the sense that the wellformedness of a sentence cannot be clearly judged from the syntactic structure alone. But given that some modern frameworks (such as HPSG) integrates the syntactic and semantic representations, a joint analysis is feasible.

Another trendy approach in deep grammar engineering is the corpus-driven approach. For instance, Miyao et al. (2004) showed that by enriching the PTB annotation with HPSG feature structures and applying top-down unifications, one can automatically acquire detailed lexical templates. The similar procedure was practiced by Hockenmaier and Steedman (2005) (though in a different framework) in the creation of the CCGbank. Recently, some of these success stories have been transferred to the development of Mandarin Chinese grammars on the Penn Chinese Treebank (CTB; (Xue et al., 2005)). Nevertheless, we believe that the corpus-driven approach does not replace the need for a carefully engineered core grammar, with which the basic linguistic generalizations could be captured and consistently applied to various instantiations in the corpus. Thus, we believe that a hand-written grammar will constitute the very foundation of the deep linguistic processing.

In this paper, we report on the on-going development of a Mandarin Chinese grammar (MCG) in the framework of HPSG. With the modern grammar engineering setup, we were able to cover a

Proceedings of the 9th Workshop on Asian Language Resources, pages 18–22,
Chiang Mai, Thailand, November 12 and 13, 2011.

large number of interesting phenomena with satisfactory accuracy from both syntactic and semantic points of view. The evaluation of the grammar resource is an important aspect of the development. At the current stage, we value the correct choice of linguistic solutions to be more important than the less meaningful parsing coverage on arbitrary "gold standard" annotation. For this reason, we choose to test the core-grammar on a phenomenon-oriented test suite instead of a corpus of naturally occurring texts.

2 An HPSG Analysis of Mandarin

2.1 Design of sign & schemata

The design of the HPSG sign in MCG is compatible with the design in the LinGO Grammar Matrix. Four valcence features were employed: SUBJ for subjects, COMPS for complements, SPR for specifiers, and SPEC for back-reference from the specifier to its head. Unlike Yu et al. (2010) who separate complement list into LCOMPS and RCOMPS, we keep all complements on the same complement list (COMPS), and use an additional boolean feature $\begin{bmatrix}\text{RC} & \pm\end{bmatrix}$ to indicate whether the complement is to the right or to the left of the head.

The grammar currently contains about 20 rule schemata. It should be noted that most of these rule schemata are very general. They are be used to handle multiple types of constructions, some of which will be illustrated below.

2.2 HEAD types

The HEAD types in HPSG identify the major categories of part-of-speech for the language. The structure of MCG's HEAD type hierarchy is show in Figure 1. Worth noticing is that we have adjectives being a sub-type of predicative, so it can serve as the predicate of a sentence (similar to verb) without *"type-raising"*. A special category *coverb* is designed to cover words which share certain properties of verbs, but usually do not serve as the main predicate of a sentence, such as prepositions (在,用), BA (把), BEI (被), and resultative coverbs (e.g. 来, 开).

2.3 Topic Construction

According to Li and Thompson (1989), a topic of a sentence refers to the theme of the sentence and appears before the subject. For a better account of the semantics, we further distinguish the following types of topics and treat them separately with different schemata.

- When the sentential topic equals the subject, the composition is done with SUBJ-HEAD, with no special treatment involved
- Temporal or location topics are treated as modifiers with ADJ-HEAD
- A special rule SUBJ2-HEAD is used to fill topics headed by noun or verb into the SPR valence of the main sentence. This is also referred to as the "double subject" constructions

Yu et al. (2010) introduce an extra valence feature (TOPIC) for the topic construction. Tse and Curran (2010) distinguish two types of topics,*gap* or *non-gap*. Both solutions are rather similar to ours nonetheless.

2.4 Numeral-classifiers & demonstratives

Numeral-classifier structures are analyzed as a phrase with rule SPEC-HEAD, and they together serve as a specifier to the head noun. A feature "CL" in the HEAD type of *noun* identifies the suitable groups of classifiers. Demonstratives are also treated as specifiers to nouns (similar to the double specifier account in (Ng, 1997)), though specific word order constraints are further enforced for the correct NP structure. Both specifiers of nouns are optional. The numeral before the classifier can be optional too, unless the NP is in a subject position and no demonstrative is available (e.g. * 头 大象 爱 吃 苹果).

2.5 DE-Constructions

DE (的) is involved in two major types of phrases:

- *Associative* DE-*phrase* where a semantic relation is created to associate the NPs before and after DE. The relation is similar to (and more general than) the possessive relation
- *Nominalizing* DE-*phrase* where DE combines with the predicative phrase before it to make a nominal phrase

While the *associative* DE-*phrase* is straightforward to model, the semantics of the *nominalizing* DE-*phrase* is more intriguing. We further categorize the nominalizing DE-phrase into the following three types:

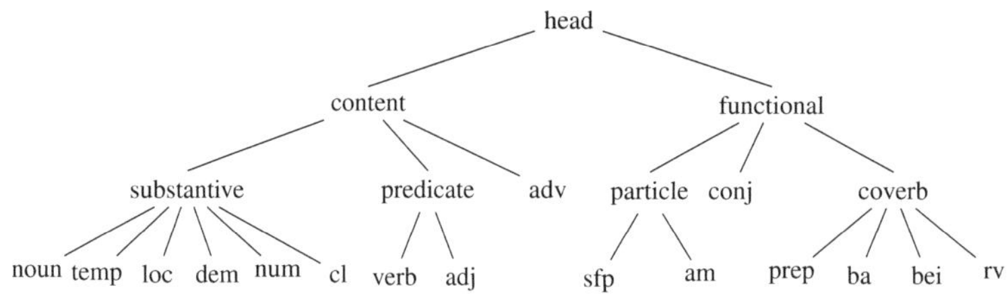

Figure 1: HEAD type hierarchy

- `subject gapping relative DE`
  where the NP after DE will serve as the subject to the predicative before DE
- `complement gapping relative DE`
  where the NP after DE will serve as the complement to the predicative before DE
- `non-gapping DE`
  where neither of the above two cases applies

Yu et al. (2010) mentioned the treatment of relative clauses using DE as a relativizer. However it is not clear whether different sub-types of the relative clauses (with different argument composition) are captured with specialized rules. Guo et al. (2007) differentiated three types of DE-constructions, ADJ-REL (relative clause), ADJUNCT (adjective), and POSS (possessive DE). We have a more fine-grained inventory for the relative clauses and treat the adjective case in the subject gapping relative DE-phrases (since we allow adjectives to be predicates, as shown in Figure 1). For example, 大 的 苹果 (big apple) will be analyzed as 大 (big) is the (adjectival) predicate of 苹果 (apple).

2.6 Locatives & temporals

Locative phrases serve as both pre-verbal and post-verbal modifiers, and generally take the form of *zai + NP + Loc*, e.g. 在 桌子 上 (on the table), 在 房子 东面 (to the east of the house), etc.

Locative phrases can always serve as pre-verbal modifiers. But only certain verbs can take post-verbal locatives with the HEAD-ADJ rule. The treatment of locative phrases as normal prepositional phrases as in (Wang et al., 2009) may lead to massive over-generation.

The analysis of temporal phrases is similar to the locative phrases.

2.7 BA-Construction

BA-construction moves the direct object of a verb to the pre-verbal position. In our analyses, we use a specialized unary rule BA-FRONTED to change the last element of the verb's complement list from $\begin{bmatrix} \text{HEAD} & \textit{noun} \\ \text{RC} & + \\ \text{INDEX} & \boxed{1} \end{bmatrix}$ to $\begin{bmatrix} \text{HEAD} & \textit{ba} \\ \text{RC} & - \\ \text{INDEX} & \boxed{1} \end{bmatrix}$.

There are various discussions on BA in the literature. Bender (2000) considered it as a verb, Gao (2000) and Wang et al. (2009) treated it as a case-marker, and Yu et al. (2010) as a preposition. We categorize BA as a special coverb. This makes it similar to prepositions. But it will be subcategorized by (instead of modifying) the verb phrase.

2.8 BEI-Construction

BEI-construction is used to compose passive voice sentences in Chinese. Similar to the analysis of BA, we use a specialized unary rule to promote the complement of the verb into the subject list, and change the original subject $\begin{bmatrix} \text{HEAD} & \textit{noun} \\ \text{INDEX} & \boxed{1} \end{bmatrix}$ into a "*bei*" headed left complement $\begin{bmatrix} \text{HEAD} & \textit{bei} \\ \text{RC} & - \\ \text{INDEX} & \boxed{1} \end{bmatrix}$.

Consistent with their analysis of BA, (Yu et al., 2010) treat BEI as a preposition. They view the complement of BEI as an extracted subject and use filler-head rule to combine the subject and the predicate. Guo et al. (2007), on the other hand, assume that the NP and VP following BEI is in one constituent, and will be case-marked by BEI jointly.

2.9 Various Markers

Several types of constructions were covered by the HEAD-MARKER/MARKER-HEAD rule, among them are the aspect markers (着, 了, 过), sentence-final particles (了, 吗), ordinal numeral prefix (第), etc. Various specific semantic information is supplemented by the marking construction.

2.10 Resultative verb compound

The resultative verb compounds refer to the compounding of a verb together with a resultative coverb (e.g., 来, 去, 开, 到, etc.), taking HEAD type *rv*, to signal the *"result"* of the action or process conveyed by the first verb. This is different to the normal modification in that the valency of the compound is mainly determined by the resultative coverb. We capture the compounding with a special RVC rule which will pass upward the head type from the first verb, and the complements from the resultative coverb.

2.11 Serial verb constructions

Serial verb construction refers to a group of complex phenomena in Mandarin Chinese where multiple verb phrases or clauses occurs in a sentence without any marker indicating the relationship between them. According to Li and Thompson (1989), it can be divided into four groups: i) two or more separate events; ii) one verb phrase or clause serving as the subject or direct object of another verb; iii) pivotal constructions; iv) descriptive clauses. We have adopted different analyses for each of them.

Yu et al. (2010) dealt mainly with the first case of the serial verb constructions. Two or more verbs were treated as coordinations, which can share subjects, topics or left-complements. Tse and Curran (2010) treated both serial verb constructions and resultative verb compound (see Section 2.10) as *verbal compounding*. Müller and Lipenkova (2009) offered more detailed theoretical analyses of certain Chinese serial verb constructions, capturing subtle semantic differences in the descriptive clauses category with additional constructional semantic relations. We intend to investigate their solutions in the future.

3 Development & Evaluation

The MCG is currently developed on the LKB platform (Copestake, 2002), which implements the typed feature structure formalism in TDL (Krieger and Schäfer, 1994). The first stage of grammar development was done with the help of the LinGO Grammar Matrix customization system, which took care of the general design of the feature geometry in HPSG, as well as the definition of the universal types for basic rule schemata and corresponding semantic compositions. Significant amount of development time were spent on the careful revision of the design and the constant debate on the treatment of various Chinese specific phenomena, while trying to keep in line with the classical HPSG theory and the conventions from other DELPH-IN grammars. As it currently stands, in addition to the types provided by the grammar Matrix, the MCG contains over 200 new type descriptions, and over 3000 lines of code in TDL. A small hand-crafted lexicon containing over 500 entries is currently used for development and testing.

Also developed is a phenomenon-oriented test suite of over 700 sentences (with both positive and negative test items). We randomly sampled 129 previously unseen sentences from the test suite and parsed them with MCG, among them are 110 wellformed sentences and 19 illformed.

		Gold standard	
		Positive	Negative
System	Positive	82	2
	Negative	28	17

Table 1: Test suite parsing performance of MCG

While the test set contains only short sentences, the phenomena are non-trivial from the linguistic view point. A sentence is considered to be successfully parse when there is a reading that is both syntactically and semantically correct. We achieve a high precision (82/84=97.6%) with an acceptable recall (82/110=74.5%). Among all negative sentences, the grammar only generated reading for two of them. One was due to the incorrect classifier constraints from a noun lexical entry. The other was due to the over-relaxed head selection in adjective+head modification. Both errors are fixed after observing the error. The parser outputs on average 5.04 readings per sentence, which attributes to the constraints we encoded in the grammar to avoid over-generation. Full coverage over phenomena such as coordinations is still lacking in MCG.

4 Summary

An overview of the MCG grammar design is presented, though the detailed presentation of our linguistic solutions does not fit in the short-paper format the workshop organizer chose for us. Nevertheless, the grammar is in line with the open-source spirit of DELPH-IN, and freely available for research purposes (http://mcg.opendfki.de/).

References

Emily M. Bender and Dan Flickinger. 2005. Rapid prototyping of scalable grammars: Towards modularity in extensions to a language-independent core. In *Proceedings of the 2nd International Joint Conference on Natural Language Processing IJCNLP-05 (Posters/Demos)*, Jeju Island, Korea.

Emily M. Bender. 2000. The syntax of mandarin ba: Reconsidering the verbal analysis. *Journal of East Asian Linguistics*, 9(2):105–145, April.

Emily M. Bender. 2008. Evaluating a crosslinguistic grammar resource: A case study of Wambaya. In *Proceedings of ACL-08: HLT*, pages 977–985, Columbus, Ohio, June. Association for Computational Linguistics.

Ann Copestake, Dan Flickinger, Carl J. Pollard, and Ivan A. Sag. 2005. Minimal recursion semantics: an introduction. *Research on Language and Computation*, 3(4):281–332.

Ann Copestake. 2002. *Implementing Typed Feature Structure Grammars*. CSLI, Stanford, USA.

Qian Gao. 2000. *Argument Structure, HPSG, and Chinese Grammar*. Ph.D. thesis, The Ohio State University.

Yuqing Guo, Josef van Genabith, and Haifeng Wang. 2007. Treebank-based acquisition of lfg resources for chinese. In *Proceedings of LFG07 Conference*, pages 214–232.

Yuqing Guo. 2009. *Treebank-Based Acquisition of Chinese LFG Resources for Parsing and Generation*. Ph.D. thesis, School of Computing, Dublin City University, July.

Julia Hockenmaier and Mark Steedman. 2005. Ccgbank: User's manual. Technical Report MS-CIS-05-09, Department of Computer and Information Science, University of Pennsylvania.

Hans-Ulrich Krieger and Ulrich Schäfer. 1994. Tdl - a type description language for constraint-based grammars. In *Proceedings of the15th International Conference on Computational Linguistics (COLING '94), August 5-9*, pages 893–899.

Charles N. Li and Sandra A. Thompson. 1989. *Mandarin Chinese: A functional reference grammar*. University of California Press, London, England.

Yusuke Miyao, Takashi Ninomiya, and Jun'ichi Tsujii. 2004. Corpus-oriented grammar development for acquiring a Head-driven Phrase Structure Grammar from the Penn Treebank. In *Proceedings of the 1st International Joint Conference on Natural Language Processing (IJCNLP 2004)*, pages 684–693, Hainan Island, China.

Stefan Müller and Janna Lipenkova. 2009. Serial verb constructions in chinese: A hpsg account. In *Proceedings of the 16th International Conference on Head-Driven Phrase Structure Grammar*, pages 234–254, Germany.

Say Kiat Ng. 1997. A double-specifier account of chinese nps using head-driven phrase structure grammar. Master's thesis, Department of Linguistics. University of Edinburgh.

Carl Pollard and Ivan A. Sag. 1994. *Head-Driven Phrase Structure Grammar*. The University of Chicago Press and CSLI Publications, Chicago, IL and Stanford, CA.

Daniel Tse and James R. Curran. 2010. Chinese ccgbank: extracting ccg derivations from the penn chinese treebank. In *Proceedings of the 23rd International Conference on Computational Linguistics (Coling 2010)*, pages 1083–1091, Beijing, China.

Xiangli Wang, Shunya Iwasawa, Yusuke Miyao, Takuya Matsuzaki, and Jun'ichi Tsujii. 2009. Design of chinese hpsg framework for data-driven parsing. In *Proceedings of the 23rd Pacific Asia Conference on Language, Information and Computation*, December.

Nianwen Xue, Fei Xia, Fu-Dong Chiou, and Martha Palmer. 2005. The penn chinese treebank: Phrase structure annotation of a large corpus. *Natural Language Engineering*, 11(02):207–238.

Kun Yu, Miyao Yusuke, Xiangli Wang, Takuya Matsuzaki, and Junichi Tsujii. 2010. Semi-automatically developing chinese hpsg grammar from the penn chinese treebank for deep parsing. In *Proceedings of the 23rd International Conference on Computational Linguistics (Coling 2010)*, pages 1417–1425, Beijing, China.

Error Detection for Treebank Validation

Bharat Ram Ambati
LTRC, IIIT-Hyderabad
ambati@research.iiit.ac.in

Rahul Agarwal
LTRC, IIIT-Hyderabad
rahul.agarwal@research.iiit.ac.in

Mridul Gupta
LTRC, IIIT-Hyderabad
mridulgp@gmail.com

Samar Husain
LTRC, IIIT-Hyderabad
samar@research.iiit.ac.in

Dipti Misra Sharma
LTRC, IIIT-Hyderabad
dipti@iiit.ac.in

Abstract

This paper describes an error detection mechanism which helps in validation of dependency treebank annotation. Consistency in treebank annotation is a must for making data as error-free as possible and for assuring the usefulness of treebank. This work is aimed at ensuring this consistency and to make the task of validation cost effective by detecting major errors induced during completely manual annotation. We evaluated our system on the Hindi dependency treebank which is currently under development. We could detect 76.63% of errors at dependency level. Results show that our system performs well even when the training data is low.

1 Introduction

For effective processing of text, tools at different conceptual levels, say from letter/syllable level to discourse level are needed. Output of these tools can then be used in different NLP based applications, beginning with simple spell checkers to sophisticated machine translation systems. These tools could be completely rule-based, statistical or hybrid systems. To build such tools, manually annotated gold standard corpora are required. Annotated corpora are mostly obtained by either manual or semi-automated processes. Hence, there are chances that errors are introduced either by human annotators or by the preprocessed output of automated tools. It is crucial that the annotated corpora are free of anomalies (errors) and inconsistencies. In the process of making these corpora error free, experts need to validate them. As the data is already annotated carefully (which is a time-consuming task), we need tools that can supplement the validators' task with a view of making the overall task fast, without compromising on reliability. With the help of such a tool, a validator can directly go to error instances and correct them. Therefore, we need the tool to have high recall. It is easy to see that a human validator can reject unintuitive errors (false positives) without much effort; one can therefore compromise a little bit on precision.

In this paper, we propose an error detection mechanism to detect dependency errors in the Hindi treebank (Bhatt et al., 2009) annotation. We classify the identified errors under specific categories for the benefit of the validators, who may choose to correct a specific type of error at one time. Though we did experiments on Hindi treebank, our approach can be applied to any under developing treebank with minimal effort.

The paper is arranged as follows. Section 2 gives a brief overview of the Hindi dependency treebank. Details of the information annotated, annotation procedure and types of possible errors in the treebank are discussed in section 3. We present the related work in section 4. In section 5, we describe our approach. Results of our approach are presented in section 6. Section 7 focuses on a general discussion about the results and approach and proposes a future direction to our work. We conclude our paper in section 8.

Proceedings of the 9th Workshop on Asian Language Resources, pages 23–30,
Chiang Mai, Thailand, November 12 and 13, 2011.

2 Hindi Dependency Treebank

A multi-layered and multi-representational treebank for Hindi (Bhatt et al., 2009; Xia et al., 2009) is being developed. The treebank will have dependency, verb-argument (PropBank, Palmer et al., 2005) and phrase structure (PS) representation. Automatic conversion from dependency structure (DS) to phrase structure (PS) is planned. Hence, it is important to have a high quality version of the dependency treebank so that the process of automated conversion to PS does not induce errors in PS. The dependency treebank contains information encoded at the morpho-syntactic (morphological, part-of-speech and chunk information) and syntactico-semantic (dependency) levels.

3 Dependency Representation

In this section we first describe the information encoded in the dependency representation of the treebank. We then briefly describe the annotation procedure for encoding this information. We also describe the possible errors at each level of annotation.

3.1 Information encoded in dependency representation

During dependency annotation, Part-Of-speech (POS), morph, chunk and inter-chunk dependency relations are annotated. Some special features are also annotated for some specific nodes. Details can be seen in this section.

Part-Of-Speech (POS) Information: POS tags are annotated for each node following the POS and chunk annotation guidelines (Bharati et al., 2006).

Morph Information: Information pertaining to the morphological features of the nodes is also encoded using the Shakti standard format (SSF) (refer, Bharati et al., 2007). These morphological features have eight mandatory feature attributes for each node. These features are classified as root, category, gender, number, person, case, post position (for a noun) or tense aspect modality (for a verb) and suffix.

Chunk Information: After annotation of POS tags, chunk boundaries are marked with appropriate assignment of chunk labels (Bharati et al., 2006). This information is also stored in SSF (Bharati et al., 2007).

Dependency Relations: After POS, morph and chunk annotation, inter-chunk dependency annotation [1] is done following the set of dependency guidelines in Bharati et al. (2009). This information is encoded at the syntactico-semantic level following the Paninian dependency framework (Begum et al., 2008; Bharati et al., 1995). After inter-chunk annotation, plan is to use a high accuracy intra-chunk expander, which marks the intra-chunk dependencies [2] and expands the chunks arriving at sentence level dependency tree.

Other Features: In the dependency treebank, apart from POS, morph, chunk and inter-chunk dependency annotations, some special features for some specific nodes are marked. For example, for the main verb of a sentential clause, information about whether the clause is declarative, interrogative or imperative is marked. Similarly, whether the sentence is in active or passive voice is also marked.

3.2 Annotation Procedure

At POS, chunk and morphological levels, corresponding state-of-the-art tools are run as a first step. An annotator then checks each node and corrects the tool's output. Another annotator (validator) takes the annotated data and validates it. At dependency level, due to unavailability of high accuracy parser, manual annotation followed by validation is done.

Annotation is being done using a tool called Sanchay[3]. Sanchay is an open source platform for working on languages, especially South Asian languages, using computers and also for developing Natural Language Processing (NLP) or other text processing applications. Apart from syntactic annotation interface (used for Hindi dependency annotation), it has several other useful functionalities as well. Font conversion, language and encoding detection, n-gram generation are a few of them.

3.3 Types of possible errors at various levels

In this section we describe the types of annotation errors at each level and provide examples for some specific types of errors.

[1] Inter-chunk dependencies are the dependency relations marked between the chunks, chunk heads to be specific.
[2] Intra-chunk dependencies are the dependency relations marked with in the chunk.
[3] http://sanchay.co.in/.

POS Errors: In POS errors we try to identify whether the Part-Of-Speech (POS) tag is correct or not for each lexical item. For example, in the example sentence given below *'chalaa'* should be the main verb (*VM*) instead of an auxiliary verb (*VAUX*).

raama	ghara	chalaa	gayaa.
NNP	NN	VAUX	VAUX
'Ram'	*'home'*	*'walk'*	*'went'*.
	"Ram went home".		

Morph Errors: Errors in the eight attribute values as mentioned in the previous section are classified as morph errors.

Chunk Errors: There can be two types of chunk errors. One is chunk type and the other is chunk boundary. In chunk type we identify whether the chunk label is correct or not. In chunk boundary we identify whether the node should belong to the same chunk or different chunk. For example, consider the following chunk,

((		NP
meraa	*'my'*	PRP
bhaaii	*'brother'*	NN
))		

In Hindi, *'meraa'* and *'bhaaii'* should be in two separate noun chunks (refer Bharati et al., 2006). So, in the above example, the chunk label of *'bhaaii'* is correct, but the boundary is wrong.

Dependency Errors: In dependency errors we try to identify whether a node is attached to its correct parent and whether its dependency label is correct or not. In addition to dependency relation errors, we also identify errors in general linguistic constraints and framework specific errors, for example, the tree well-formedness assumption in dependency analysis. Framework specific example would be that children of a conjunct should be of similar type (Bharati et al., 2009). For example, a conjunct can have two nouns as its children but not a noun and a verb as its children.

Other Feature Errors: Errors in the special features discussed above are classified under other feature errors.

Focus of the current paper is to describe the methodology employed to detect errors in the dependency level (inter-chunk dependencies) of the DS representation. Error detection at intra-chunk dependencies is out of scope of this paper. In the rest of the paper, by dependency level, we mean inter-chunk dependencies unless explicitly stated. In the following section, we first describe the related work in the area of detecting errors in treebanks, in general. Then, we present the work on Hindi in particular.

4 Related Work:

Validation and correction tools are an important part for making treebanks error-free and consistent. With an increase in demand for high quality annotated corpora over the last decade, major research works in the field of developing lexical resources have focused on detection of errors.

One such approach for treebank error detection has been employed by Dickinson and Meurers (2003a; 2003b; 2005) and Boyd et al. (2008). The underlying principle in these works is to detect "variation n-grams" in syntactic annotation across large corpora. These variations could be present for a continuous sequence of words (POS and chunks) or for a non-continuous sequence of words (dependency structures), more the number of variation for a particular contiguous or non-contiguous sequence of tokens (or words), greater the chance of the particular variation being an error. They use these statistical patterns (n-grams) to detect anomalies in POS annotation in corpora such as the Penn treebank (Marcus et al., 1993), TIGER corpus (Brants et al., 2002) etc. For discontinuous patterns as found most commonly in dependency annotation (Boyd et al., 2008), they tested their strategy on Talbanken05 (Nivre et al., 2006) apart from the corpora mentioned above. This we believe was the first mainstream work on error detection in dependency annotation.

Some other earlier methods employed for error detection in syntactic annotation (mainly POS and chunk), are by Eskin (2000) and van Halteren (2000). Based on large corpora, van Noord (2004) and de Kok et al. (2009) employed error mining techniques. The basic underlying strategy was to obtain a set of parsed and un-parsed sentences using a wide-coverage parser and compute suspicion ratio for detecting errors. Other examples of detection of annotation errors in treebanks include Kaljurand (2004) and Kordoni (2003).

Most of the aforementioned techniques work well with large corpora in which the frequency of occurrence of words is very high. Hence, none of them account for data sparsity except for de Kok et al. (2009). Moreover, the techniques employed by van Noord (2004) and de Kok et al. (2009) rely on the output of a reliable state-of-the-art parser which may not be available for many languages just as in the case of Hindi, the language in question for our work.

It becomes a challenge to develop error detection tools for small treebanks like Hindi. There is an effort by Ambati et al. (2010) in this direction for Hindi treebank validation. They used a combination of a rule-based and hybrid system to detect treebank errors. Rule-based system works on the development of robust (high precision) rules which are formed using the annotation guidelines and the framework, whereas the hybrid system is a combination of statistical module with a rule-based post-processing module. The statistical module helps in detecting a wide array of potential errors and suspect cases. The rule-based post-processing module then prunes out the false positives, with the help of robust and efficient rules thereby ensuring higher precision value.

Note that both "Rule-Based Approach" and "Rule-based post-processing" modules have separate goals. Goal of "Rule-Based Approach" is to detect errors using high precision rules. Whereas goal for the later, is to prune the false positives given by the statistical approach. Former one tries to increase the precision of the system, whereas the later tries to increase the recall of the system. Rules used in "Rule-Based Approach" can be used in post-processing module, but vice versa is not true. The entire framework is sketched in Figure 1.

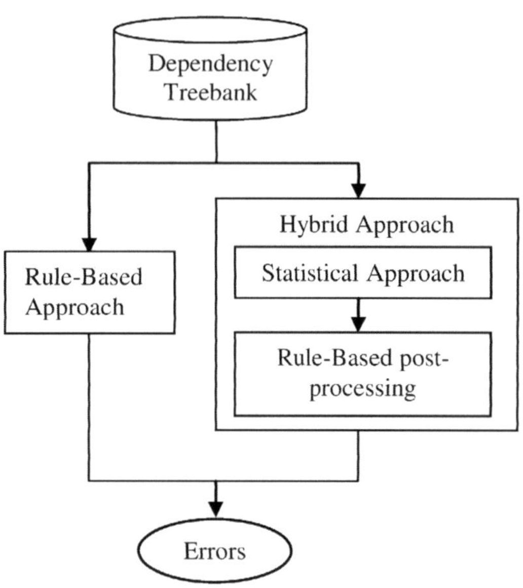

Figure 1. Error detection framework by Ambati et al. (2010)

Ambati et al. (2010) could detect errors in POS and chunk annotations with reasonable accuracies. But at dependency level recall of overall system (combination of rule-based and hybrid approaches) is 40.33% only. This is mainly due to low performance of the statistical module. In statistical module, they extracted frequencies of child and parent node bi-grams in the dependency tree. To handle scarcity issues, they explored different similarity measures and merged similar patterns. We call this as "Frequency Based Statistical Module (FBSM)". Major limitation of this approach is that one cannot give richer context due to the problem of scarcity. To find whether the dependency label is correct or not, apart from node and its parent information, contextual features like sibling and child information is also helpful. Current state-of-the-art dependency parsers like MSTParser[4] and MaltParser[5] use these features for dependency labeling (McDonald et al., 2006; Nivre et al., 2007; Kosaraju et al., 2010). Finding similarity between patterns and merging similar patterns would not help when we wish to take a much richer context.

In this paper, we propose a probability based statistical module (PBSM) to overcome this problem of FBSM. With this approach, we evaluate and compare the performance of PBSM and FBSM. Now in place of FBSM, we integrate PBSM into overall system of Ambati et al. (2010) and compare the results.

5 Our Approach: Probability Based Statistical Module (PBSM):

In this probability based statistical module, we first extract the contextual features which help in identifying the correct tag. For example, at the dependency level, apart from node and its parent features, sibling and child features with their respective dependency labels are very useful in predicting the correct dependency label. Using these contextual features from the training data, we create a model using maximum entropy classification algorithm[6] (MAXENT). This model gives the probabilities of all possible output tags (here dependency labels) for a given context. For each node in the test data, we first extract the context information and the input tag of that node. We then extract the list of all possible dependency tags with their probabilities for this

[4] http://sourceforge.net/projects/mstparser/
[5] http://maltparser.org/
[6] http://maxent.sourceforge.net/

context using the trained model. From this list we extract first best and second best tags and their corresponding probabilities.

If the input tag doesn't match with the first best tag, and if the probability of the first best tag is greater than a particular threshold, we then consider it as a possible error node. These could be valid errors or the cases which require much richer context to find the correct tag.

If both the input tag and the first best tag given by the model match, we then fix a maximum and minimum threshold on the probability values. If the probability of the first best tag is greater than the maximum threshold, we do not consider it as a potential error. The chance of it being an error is very low as the system is very confident about its decision. If the probability of the first best tag is less than the minimum threshold, it is considered as a possible error. This could either be the case of an error pattern or a correct but less frequent pattern. If it is the latter, then the rule-based post-processing tool will remove this false positive.

If the probability value lies between the maximum and minimum thresholds, we calculate the difference between the probabilities of the first and second best tags. If the difference is less than a particular value, it means that there is high ambiguity between these two tags. As there is high ambiguity there is a greater chance of making an error. Hence, we identify this case as a possible error. In this way using the probabilistic approach, we not only detect the possible errors, but also classify them into different categories.

find_errors (input)

```
    for each sentence in the input:
      for each node in the sentence:
1.      Get the node's context
2.      Get the input_tag
3.      tags_probs = get_probabilities(context);
4.      1stBestTag = tags_probs[0][0];
5.      1stBestProb = tags_probs[0][1];
6.      2ndBestTag = tags_probs[1][0];
7.      2ndBestProb = tags_probs[1][1];
8.      if input_tag != 1stBestTag:
          if 1stBestProb > thres_minX:
            mark node as error node (less context);
9.      else:
          if 1stBestProb < thres_max:
            if 1stBestProb < thres_min:
              mark node as error node (less frequent);
            else if 1stBestProb-2ndBestProb < thres_dif:
              mark node as error node (ambiguous);
```

get_probabilities(context)

```
1.  Load the trained maxent model
2.  Predict probabilities of all tags for the context.
3.  Store the tags and their probabilities in an array.
4.  Return the array.
```

Figure 2. Algorithm employed for PBSM

Figure 2 shows the algorithm of probability based statistical module (PBSM). Use of richer contextual information and probabilities to detect errors makes this approach more effective from the previous approaches employed for error detection (Dickinson and Meurers, 2003a; 2003b; 2005; Boyd et al., 2008; Ambati et al., 2010).

Using this approach, not only can one detect errors but also classify them under specific categories like less context, less frequent and ambiguous cases, which will help the validation process. This helps the validators to correct the errors in a focused way. For example, a validator can check and correct all the error in "less frequent" category first and then start correcting "ambiguous cases". It also helps validator to decide the amount of energy he/she needs to spend. For example, correcting "ambiguous cases" would require more time compared to other categories. This could be because the validator might look for sentence or sometimes discourse level information to resolve the ambiguity. He/she could also contact peers or an expert to resolve it. Hence, more time might be required to resolve "ambiguous cases" compared to others.

6 Experiments and Results

We used same data used by Ambati et al. (2010) for evaluation. This is a 65k-token manually annotated and validated sample of data (2694 sentences) derived from the Hindi dependency treebank. The data is divided into 40k, 10k and 15k for training, development and testing respectively. We used training data to train the model and development data to tune the parameters like threshold values. For our experiments, *thres_max*= 0.8, *thres_min* = 0.2, *thres_minX* = 0.25 and *thres_dif* = 0.25 gave the best performance.

Table 1 shows the performance of PBSM and compares it with FBSM. FBSM of Ambati et al. (2010) could identify only 18.74% of the dependency errors. The precision recorded for this approach was also quite low. But with our PBSM, we could detect 57.06% of the dependency errors with a reasonable precision value. Note that, our main aim is to achieve a high recall value. The false positives can be easily discarded by the validators.

Approach	Total Errors (Total instances)	System output	Correct Errors	Recall
FBSM of Ambati et al. (2010)	843 (7113)	2546	158	18.74%
PBSM: Our Approach	843 (7113)	2000	481	57.06%

Table 1. Error detection at dependency level using FBSM of Ambati et al. (2010) and our PBSM

Overall system recall of Ambati et al. (2010) for error detection at dependency level is 40.33%. This system uses FBSM in hybrid approach. We replaced FBSM with our PBSM and re-evaluated the overall system of Ambati et al. (2010). The modified system could achieve a recall of 76.63% with reasonable precision of 29.84%. Results are shown in Table 2.

Approach	Total Errors	System output	Correct Errors	Recall
Ambati et al. (2010) overall system with FBSM	843	2728	340	40.33%
Ambati et al. (2010) overall system with PBSM	843	2165	646	76.63%

Table 2. Error Detection at dependency level using overall system of Ambati et al. (2010) with FBSM and PBSM

7 Discussion and Future work

Proposed PBSM identifies 38% more errors than the FBSM at dependency level. As we have less data, hypothesis for FBSM, "Low frequency is a possible sign of error", didn't work. Unsurprisingly, several valid patterns had low counts. Major advantage of PBSM over FBSM is the use of richer context. Richer context helped PBSM to predict the errors more accurately. But in FBSM we couldn't use it because of sparsity issues. Results show that our approach works well even when the size of the data is low.

The tool is being constantly improved. We are analyzing the errors which are missed out and planning to improve. Currently, precision of the system is low. Improving the "Rule-based post-processing" step of hybrid approach can significantly increase the precision. We can build an interface where a validator while validating the data can automatically add new rules to this post-processing step. We would also like to evaluate our system on the time taken for validation. That is the reduction in the validation time using this system. We are also planning to build a user-friendly interface which helps validators in correcting the errors.

This system can also help in improving the guidelines which subsequently improves the annotation. While correcting the errors if the validator comes across some ambiguous decisions or some common errors or comes up with new decisions, guidelines can be modified accordingly to reflect the changes. Data annotated based on new guidelines will reduce the occurrence of these errors and eventually the quality of annotation of individual as well as entire data will improve.

Figure 3, shows the complete cycle of this process.

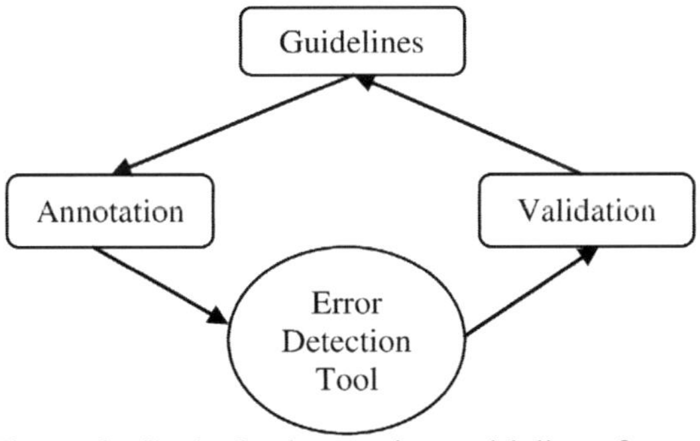

Figure 3. Cycle for improving guidelines for annotation

Although we worked and presented our results only on the Hindi Treebank, our approach can be generalized to any language and to any framework. Parameter tuning like the threshold values is the only part which depend on the size of data, language and the framework.

8 Conclusions

We proposed a novel approach to detect errors in the treebanks. This approach can significantly reduce the validation time. We tested it on Hindi dependency treebank data and were able to detect 76.63% of errors at dependency level. This tool can be generalized to detect errors in annotation of any language/framework. Results show that the proposed approach works well even when the size of the data is low.

References

B. R. Ambati, M. Gupta, S. Husain and D. M. Sharma. 2010. A high recall error identification tool for Hindi treebank validation. In *Proceedings of The 7th International Conference on Language Resources and Evaluation (LREC), Valleta, Malta.*

R. Begum, S. Husain, A. Dhwaj, D. M. Sharma, L. Bai, and R. Sangal. 2008. Dependency annotation scheme for Indian languages. In *Proceedings of IJCNLP-2008.*

A. Bharati, V. Chaitanya and R. Sangal. 1995. *Natural Language Processing: A Paninian Perspective, Prentice-Hall of India, New Delhi,* pp. 65-106.

A. Bharati, R. Sangal, D. M. Sharma and L. Bai. 2006. AnnCorra: Annotating Corpora Guidelines for POS and Chunk Annotation for Indian Languages. *Technical Report (TR-LTRC-31), Language Technologies Research Centre, IIIT-Hyderabad.*

A. Bharati, R. Sangal and D. M. Sharma. 2007. SSF: Shakti Standard Format Guide. *Technical Report (TR-LTRC-33), LTRC, IIIT-Hyderabad.*

A. Bharati, D. M. Sharma S. Husain, L. Bai, R. Begam and R. Sangal. 2009. AnnCorra: TreeBanks for Indian Languages, Guidelines for Annotating Hindi TreeBank (version – 2.0). http://ltrc.iiit.ac.in/MachineTrans/research/tb/DS-guidelines/DS-guidelines-ver2-28-05-09.pdf

R. Bhatt, B. Narasimhan, M. Palmer, O. Rambow, D. M. Sharma and F. Xia. 2009. Multi-Representational and Multi-Layered Treebank for Hindi/Urdu. In *Proc. of the Third Linguistic Annotation Workshop at 47th ACL and 4th IJCNLP.*

A. Boyd, M. Dickinson, and W. D. Meurers. 2008. On Detecting Errors in Dependency Treebanks. *Research on Language and Computation* 6(2), pp. 113-137.

S. Brants, S. Dipper, S. Hansen, W. Lezius and G. Smith, 2002. The TIGER Treebank. In *Proceedings of TLT-02.* Sozopol, Bulgaria.

M. Dickinson and W. D. Meurers. 2003a. Detecting Inconsistencies in Treebank. In *Proc. of the Second Workshop on Treebanks and Linguistic Theories (TLT 2003).*

M. Dickinson and W. D. Meurers. 2003b. Detecting Errors in Part-of-Speech Annotation. In *Proceedings of the 10th Conference of the European Chapter of the Association for Computational Linguistics (EACL-03).* Budapest, pp. 107–114.

M. Dickinson and W. D. Meurers. 2005. Detecting Errors in Discontinuous Structural Annotation. In *Proc. of the 43rd Annual Meeting of the ACL,* pp. 322–329.

E. Eskin. 2000. Automatic Corpus Correction with Anomaly Detection. In *Proceedings of the First Conference of the North American Chapter of the-Association for Computational Linguistics (NAACL-00).* Seattle, Washington.

Hans van Halteren. 2000. The Detection of Inconsistency in Manually Tagged Text. In *Proceedings of the 2ndWorkshop on Linguistically Interpreted Corpora.* Luxembourg.

K. Kaljurand. 2004. Checking treebank consistency to find annotation errors. http://math.ut.ee/~kaarel/NLP/Programs/Treebank/ConsistencyChecking/

Daniel de Kok, Jianqiang Ma and Gertjan van Noord. 2009. A generalized method for iterative error mining in parsing results. In *Proceedings of Workshop on Grammar Engineering Across Frameworks (GEAF 2009), 47th ACL – 4th IJCNLP,* Singapore.

V. Kordoni. 2003. Strategies for annotation of large corpora of multilingual spontaneous speech data. In *Proc. of Workshop on Multilingual Corpora: Lin-*

guistic Requirements and Technical Perspectives held at Corpus Linguistics 2003.

P. Kosaraju, S. R. Kesidi, V. B. R. Ainavolu and P. Kukkadapu. 2010. Experiments on Indian Language Dependency Parsing. In *Proceedings of the ICON10 NLP Tools Contest: Indian Language Dependency Parsing.*

M. P. Marcus, M. A. Marcinkiewicz, B. Santorini. 1993. Building a large annotated corpus of English: the Penn treebank. *Computational Linguistics, Volume 19,* Issue 2 (313 – 330).

R. McDonald, K. Lerman, and F. Pereira. 2006. Multilingual dependency analysis with a two-stage discriminative parser. In *Proceedings of the Tenth Conference on Computational Natural Language Learning (CoNLL-X),* pp. 216–220.

J. Nivre, J. Hall, J. Nilsson, A. Chanev, G. Eryigit, S. Kübler, S. Marinov and E Marsi. 2007. *MaltParser: A language-independent system for data-driven dependency parsing. Natural Language Engineering,* 13(2), 95-135.

J. Nivre, J. Nilsson and J. Hall. 2006. Talbanken05: A Swedish Treebank with Phrase Structure and Dependency Annotation. In *Proceedings of the fifth international conference on Language Resources and Evaluation (LREC- 06).* Genoa, Italy.

Gertjan van Noord. 2004. Error Mining for Wide-Coverage Grammar Engineering. In *Proceedings of ACL 2004,* Barcelona, Spain.

M. Palmer, D. Gildea, P. Kingsbury. 2005. The Proposition Bank: An Annotated Corpus of Semantic Roles. *Computational Linguistics, 31(1):*71-106.

F. Xia, O. Rambow, R. Bhatt, M. Palmer, and D. M. Sharma. 2009. Towards a Multi-Representational Treebank. In *Proceedings of the 7th International Workshop on Treebanks and Linguistic Theories (TLT 2009),* Groningen, Netherlands.

Experiences in building the Urdu WordNet

Farah Adeeba
Center for Language Engineering
Al-Khawazmi Institute of Computer Science
University of Engineering and Technology
Lahore
farah.adeeba@kics.edu.pk

Sarmad Hussain
Center for Language Engineering
Al-Khawazmi Institute of Computer Science
University of Engineering and Technology
Lahore
Sarmad.hussain@kics.edu.pk

Abstract

This paper attempts to report on developing a WordNet for Urdu on the basis of Hindi WordNet. The resource currently contains about 50000 unique words organized in 28967 synsets. The paper also discusses the problems encountered along the way of transliteration from Hindi WordNet and manual cleaning. It concludes with the planned future work.

1 Introduction

WordNet is one of the useful and important lexical resources based on the formalisms developed in lexical semantics. It defines different senses associated with the meaning of a word and other well-defined lexical relations such as synonyms, antonyms, hypernym, hyponyms, meronyms and holonyms. WordNet is used for many natural language processing and computational linguistic tasks such as Word Sense Disambiguation, Word Similarity, Information Retrieval and Extraction and Machine Translation, etc.

The motivation for the creation of Urdu WordNet is to provide a lexical resource that can be used as a tool for enhancing the performance of machine translation and information retrieval. We have attempted to provide a basic resource that can be used in above mentioned NLP applications. As the manual construction of Urdu WordNet from scratch would be very costly and time consuming, we have used the WordNet expansion approach. Lexical information is extracted from Hindi WordNet due to similarity between two languages.

Hindi and Urdu are grammatically similar languages but written in two dissimilar scripts Devanagri and Arabic respectively. These languages share a large number of words, morphology, vocabulary, and cultural heritage. It is easier for both speakers to verbally understand each other but they face the barrier of different script incase of written expression. Hindi and Urdu are spoken by more than 60 million people in India and Pakistan (Language Summary, http://www.ethnologue.com/ethno_docs/distribution.asp?by=size).

The roadmap for the rest of paper is as follows: Section 2 discusses Hindi and Urdu Scripts along Hindi WordNet. Methodology for development of Urdu WordNet is described in Section 3 and statistics of system is given in Section 4. The current status and future work is discussed in Section 5. Finally section 6 concludes the paper.

2 Literature Overview

Urdu (اردو) is written in Persio-Arabic script and normally in Nastaliqb writing style (Hussain, 2004). It is a right-to-left script and the shape of character differ depending on its position in word i.e. shape of character would be different in initial, middle, and end of word. Urdu is written in bidirectional form i.e. letters are written from right-to-left and numbers from left-to-right format. Urdu is written with consonantal letters and aerabs. The vocalic content is specified by using the aerab with letters. Aerab position can be on the top and bottom of letter. A sentence illustrating Urdu is given below:

اردو عربی رسم الخط میں لکھی جاتی ہے۔

(Urdu Arbi Rasm-ul-Khat mein likhi jati hay)
(Urdu is written in Arabic script)

Hindi (हिन्दी) is written in Devanagri script, descended from the Brahmi script. It is the simplified version of Sanskrit, written in left-to-

Proceedings of the 9th Workshop on Asian Language Resources, pages 31–35,
Chiang Mai, Thailand, November 12 and 13, 2011.

right direction. In Hindi each consonant letter by default inherits vowel which can be altered or muted by means of diacritics or matra. Vowels can be written as independent letters or by using a diacritic marks. Two or more consonants may occur together in clusters called Conjunct. A sentence written in Hindi is given below.

हिन्दी हिंदूस्तान की कौमी ज़बान है.

(Hindi India ki Quomi Zuban hay)

(Hindi is the national language of India)

Hindi WordNet (HWN) is lexical database inspired by the English WordNet (Miller, 1993).The words in HWN are grouped together according to their similarity of meanings. Two words that can be interchanged in a context are synonymous in that context. Synsets or the synonym sets are the basic building blocks of HWN. For each word there is a synonym set, or synsets representing one lexical concept. There are 10 relations in HWN; Synonymy, Hypernymy / Hyponymy, Antonymy, Meronymy / Holonymy, Gradation, Entailment, Troponymy and Causative (Dipak , 2002). The Hindi WordNet deals only with the open class words. Thus, HWN contains the following categories of words. The details of Hindi WordNet are given in Table 1.

Category	Count
Noun	56623
Verbs	3894
Adjectives	13702
Adverbs	1276
Synsets	30977

Table 1: Hindi WordNet

Hindi WordNet is used as a pivot WordNet for building WordNet of Ando-Aryan languages eg. Marathi WordNet, Sanskrit WordNet (Kulkarni, 2010), Nepali WordNet (Chakrabarty, 2006) , Bengali WordNet. The Expansion Approach of WordNet (Vossen, 2002) creation is used as method for creation of a new Word Nets. This expansion approach is also being used for development of Urdu WordNet by Tafseer et.al (Tafseer Ahmed, 2010).

They developed Urdu WordNet by extracting information contained in existing Hindi WordNet. To overcome the scriptural barrier they used transliteration. The lexical information is obtained by using the Hindi WordNet API. The gloss with the example sentence and the synset description is left out into Urdu WordNet.

3 Methodology

Because of the high degree of similarity between the Urdu and Hindi, we have picked up the Hindi WordNet as the pivot WordNet. The HWN offline version of 2.1 is being used that provides information of synset and senses. The Hindi WordNet database is picked up from (http://www.cfilt.iitb.ac.in/wordnet/webhwn/do wnloaderInfo.php) and transliterated it into Urdu. Hindi to Urdu WordNet conversion process is shown in Figure 1.

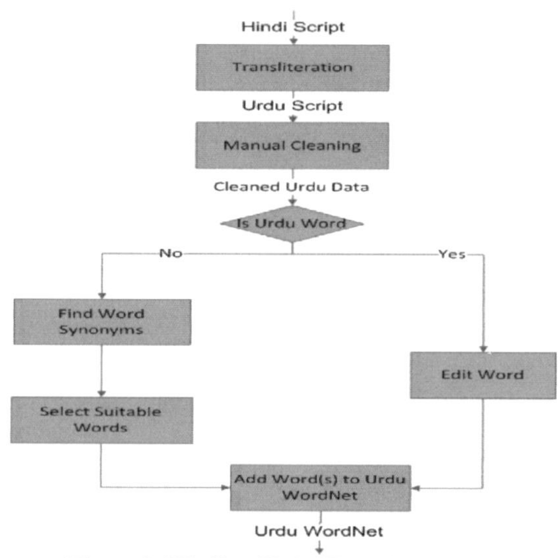

Figure 1: Hindi to Urdu WordNet Conversion

For the automatic transliteration we have developed the software which transliterates the Hindi script into Urdu script. For mapping of Hindi consonants, and vowels into Urdu number of rules are used depending on the position in the word i.e. same Hindi vowel would be mapped to different Urdu characters at the start, middle, and at the end of word e.g. ə is mapped to Alef (ا) + Zabar َ at the start of a word and by Zabar َ in the middle of a word. These rules are discussed in (Abbas Malik, 2008).

The transliteration system does not resolve the problem of multi-equivalences. For example the Hindi 'त' can be mapped to 'ت' *(Tay)* and 'ط'*(Tuay)*. A list of multi-equivalence Hindi character is given in Table 2.

The multi-equivalence problem from Hindi to Urdu transliteration is problematic which needs to be solved. An automated method is applied to resolve this by analyzing the Urdu character frequency using an Urdu corpus i.e. to resolve the above problem the system map 'त' to 'ت' *(Tay)* due to more frequency of 'ت'*(Tay)* as compared to 'ط'*(Tuay)*.

Hindi	Urdu
अ	آ،ا *(Alif-Mad, Alif)*
त	ط،ت *(Tuay, Tay)*
स	ص،س،ث *(Suad, Seen, Say)*
ह	ہ،ح *(Hay)*
ज़	ظ،ض،ژ،ذ،ز *(Zueen, Zuad, Yeh, Zaal, Zeh)*
क	ک،ق *(Kaf)*

Table 2: Multiple Urdu characters for one Hindi character

Afterwards, multi-equivalence problem is resolved manually by analyzing the text.
Although Hindi and Urdu are grammatically similar languages and share a large number of words, morphology, vocabulary and cultural heritage. But still there are number of Hindi words that are not used in Urdu. Therefore there is need to remove the Hindi words like انتیرن *(Anteeran)* (अंतीरन, fail) from Urdu WordNet. There are two steps to do this First find out the corresponding Urdu word and Second discard original Hindi Word. The deletion of Hindi word is shown in Figure 2.

ID :: 83
CAT :: adjective
CONCEPT :: जो परीक्षा में उत्तीर्ण न हुआ हो
EXAMPLE :: "रोहन परीक्षा में अनुत्तीर्ण हो गया"
SYNSET-HINDI :: अनुत्तीर्ण,फेल

Hindi WordNet Entry

ID :: 83
CAT :: adjective
CONCEPT :: جو پریکشا میں انتیرن نہ ہوا ہو
(Jo priksha mein Antteeran na huwa ho)
(Failed in exam)
EXAMPLE :: ""روہن پریکشا میں انتیرن ہو گیا
(Rohan priksha mein Antteeran ho gaya)
(Rohan has failed the test)
SYNSET-URDU :: انتیرن،فیل
(Anteeran , Fail)
(Fail)

Urdu WordNet Entry after Transliteration

ID :: 83
CAT :: adjective
CONCEPT :: امتحان میں ناکامیاب
(Imtihan mein nakamyab)
(Failed in exam)
EXAMPLE :: "روہن امتحان میں فیل ہو گیا"
(Rohan Imtihan mein fail ho gaya)
(Rohan has failed the test)
SYNSET-URDU :: فیل،ناکام
(Fail, Nakam)
(Fail)

Final Urdu WordNet Entry

Figure 2: Hindi Word to Urdu Word

Similarly, numbers of Urdu words are added in database, which are not present in Hindi WordNet. For example the word ربا (interest) is added in Urdu WordNet. The entry of ربا is shown in Figure 3.

ربا (Riba)
ID :: 7350
CAT :: noun
CONCEPT :: وہ رقم جو اصل پر زائد وصول کی جائے
(Woh raqam jo asal par zaid wasol ki jayey)
(The amount charged but more than the actual amount)
EXAMPLE :: ""اسلام میں ربا حرام ہے
(Islam mein Riba Haram Hai)
(Interest is forbidden in Islam)
SYNSET-URDU :: ربا،سود،بیاج
(Riba, Sood, Biyaj)
(Interest)

Figure 3: Sample New Word Added in Urdu WordNet

4 Urdu WordNet

The UWN currently has around 28967 synsets consisting of nouns, verbs, adverbs and adjectives. The detail of WordNet is shown in Table 3.

Category	Count
Noun	48224
Verb	3000
Adverb	705
Adjective	8000
Unique Words	50000
Synset	28967

Table 3: Urdu WordNet

Since it is currently in development phase so, new synset will get introduced in UWN. The front-end of the tool has been implemented in .NET. The application interface is connected at the backend with text files of synsets. The data is divided into 4 files i.e. Urdu-common, Urdu-core, Urdu-full and English. The synset entry format in file is shown in Figure 4.

ID: The synset identifier.
CAT: The syntactic category of the sense.
CONCEPT: It explains the concept represented by the synset.
EXAMPLE: It gives the usage of the words of the synsets in the sentence
SYNSET-URDU: It gives the set of synonyms for the sense in the Urdu language

Figure 4: Synset Entry Format

At present the offline version of Urdu WordNet is available which can be made available online after proper security implementation.

5 Discission & Future Work

This paper presents experience of building Urdu WordNet by Using the Hindi WordNet. The current Urdu WordNet does not provide the full-fledged lexical information of Urdu Words but, it can be used to extract the sense and synset information.

Although new Urdu words are added in Urdu WordNet which were missing in Hindi WordNet. Still there is need to add more Persian and Arabic load Urdu words to cover vocabulary of Urdu.

Diacritics are partially handled in Urdu WordNet. Currently there is no clear distinction between two words which have same written expression in case of no diacritic e.g. the بَنا *(ban-na)(making)* and word بُنا *(bun-na)(knitting)* are written as بنا *(ban-na)* in Urdu WordNet. The details of these words are given in Figure 4 & Figure 5. The Urdu WordNet system needs to be mature enough to handle diacritics. This can be achieved by adding up the diacritics in Urdu WordNet database.

ID :: 7132
CAT :: verb
CONCEPT :: روپ دینا
(Roop Dena)
(Form in a shape)
EXAMPLE :: "مندر بن گیا ہے"
(Mandir Bun gaya hai)
(The temple has constructed)
SYNSET-URDU :: بننا، تیار ہونا
(Ban-na , Tyar hona)

Figure 5: WordNet Entry for بنا (ban-na) (make)

ID :: 7310
CAT :: verb
CONCEPT :: ہاتھ یا اوزاروں سے کچھ سوتوں کو اوپر اور کچھ کو نیچے سے نکال کر کوئی چیز بنانا
(Haath ya ozaron sey kuch soton ko ooper aur kuch ko nechey sy nikal ker koi cheez banana)
(Made something with the help of hand or tools by springs up and down)
EXAMPLE :: سیتا اپنے بچے کے لئے ایک سویٹر بن رہی "ہے"
(Seeta Apney betey kay liyey saweeter bun rahi hai)
(Sitta is knitting a sweeter for her baby)
SYNSET-URDU :: بننا، بنائی کرنا
(bun-na, bunaye karna)
(Knitting)

Figure 6: WordNet Entry for بنا (bun-na)(Knitting)

The semantic relations such like antonymy, hypernymy, hyponymy, me-ronymy, holonymy, troponymy, entailment etc. are ignored in Urdu WordNet. These relationships can be added to provide complete lexical information of Word.

The extension of Urdu WordNet further involves work in the area of compound words especially in the implementation of complex predicates e.g.

نکل گیا *(nikle gaya) (went out)*. In Urdu 20% verb forms in the running text are compound verbs (Compound Verb, http://en.wikipedia.org/wiki/Compound_verb). So, there is need to add complex predicates which are used more frequently than normal verb.

Currently Compound words (Noun, adverbs) e.g. آہستہ آہستہ *(Ahista Ahista) (slowely Slowely)* are joined using "–"instead of Zero Width noun-joiner. There is need to add mechanism into WordNet tool to handle this issue.

6 Conclusion

In this paper, we present a report on development of Urdu WordNet by extracting information contained in existing Hindi WordNet. The scriptural barrier between two languages is crossed by using automatic and manual transliteration. Despite the similarity between two languages, concept translation is employed to remove Hindi words from Urdu WordNet. New Urdu words are also added in WordNet which are not present in Hindi WordNet.

Acknowledgements
We would like to thank Hindi WordNet Group at IIT Bombay for their support and especially Prof. Pushpak Bhattacharyya, Laxmi Kashyap, Salil Joshi, and Prabhakar Pandey. We acknowledge Asad Mustafa CLE-KICS for helping us in Urdu translation.

References

M. G. Abbas Malik , Christian Boitet , Pushpak Bhattacharyya, *Hindi Urdu machine transliteration using finite-state transducers*, Proceedings of the 22nd International Conference on Computational Linguistics, p.537-544, August 18-22, 2008, Manchester, United Kingdom

"Language Summary" Reterived July 2011 from, http://www.ethnologue.com/ethno_docs/distribution.asp?by=size

"Word Net Applications" Reterived July 2011 from, http://en.wikipedia.org/wiki/WordNet#Applications

Dipak Narayan, Debasri Chakrabarti, Prabhakar Pande and P. Bhattacharyya, *An Experience in Building the Indo WordNet - a WordNet for Hindi*, First International Conference on Global WordNet, Mysore, India, January 2002.

"Hindi WordNet" Reterived July 2011 from http://www.cfilt.iitb.ac.in/wordnet/webhwn/wn.php

"Hindi Word Net" Reterived July 2011 from, http://www.cfilt.iitb.ac.in/wordnet/webhwn/downloaderInfo.php

Hussain, Sarmad. 2004. *Letter-to-Sound Rules for Urdu Test to Speech System*, Proceeding of workshop on computational Approaches to Arabic Script-based Languages, COLING 2004, Geneva, Switzerland.

George A. Miller, Richard Beckwith, Christiane Fellbaum,Derek Gross, and Katherine J. Miller. 1993.*Five Papers on WordNet*. MIT press. http://www.mit.edu/~6.863/spring2009/readings/5papers.pdf

P.Vossen. 2002 Euro WordNet: General Document. University of Amesterdam

"Compound Verb" Reterived July 2011 from http://en.wikipedia.org/wiki/Compound_verb

Pushpak Bhattacharyya, *IndoWordNet*, Lexical Resources Engineering Conference 2010 (LREC 2010), Malta, May, 2010.

Debasri Chakrabarti, Vaijayanthi Sarma and Pushpak Bhattacharyya. 2007. *Complex Predicates in Indian Language* Wordnets, Lexical Resources and Evaluation Journal, 40 (3--4).

Tafseer Ahmed and Annette Hautli (2010). *Developing a Basic Lexical Resource for Urdu Using Hindi WordNet*. Proceedings of CLT10, Islamabad, Pakistan.

Alok Chakrabarty, Bipul Purkayastha and Arindam Roy. *Experiences In Building The Nepali Wordnet - Insights And Challenges*. The Fifth Global Wordnet Conference @ CFILT, IIT Bombay, Mumbai

Malhar Kulkarni, et al. (2010). *Introducing Sanskrit Wordnet*. The 5th International Conference of the Global WordNet Association (GWC-2010), 31st Jan - 4th Feb, 2010,

Feasibility of Leveraging Crowd Sourcing for the Creation of a Large Scale Annotated Resource for Hindi English Code Switched Data: A Pilot Annotation

Mona Diab
Center for Computational Learning Systems
Columbia University, New York
mdiab@ccls.columbia.edu

Ankit Kamboj
Computer Science Dept.
Columbia University, New York
ak3171@columbia.edu

Abstract

Linguistic code switching (LCS) occurs when speakers mix multiple languages in the same speech utterance. We find LCS pervasively in bilingual communities. LCS poses a serious challenge to Natural Language and Speech Processing. With the ubiquity of informal genres online, LCS is emerging as a very widespread phenomenon. This paper presents a first attempt at collecting and annotating a large repository of LCS data. We target Hindi English (Hinglish) LCS. We investigate the feasibility of leveraging crowd sourcing as a means for annotating the data on the word level. This paper briefly explains the setup of the experiment and data collection. It also presents statistics representing agreements among annotators over different possible categories of Hinglish words and analyzes the confidence with which a code switched word can be annotated in the correct category by humans.

1 Introduction

Linguistic Code switching (LCS) is the term used to describe a common practice among bilingual speakers of a given language pair in which the speakers switch back and forth between their common languages. This phenomenon is dominantly observed in inhabitants of countries like India where Hindi is a common first language (L1) and English acts as a second language (L2) among native Hindi speakers. For example, the following Hindi sentence with code switches to English is a seamless example of North Indian conversation: ***Uske*** *communication* ***ki wajah se hi*** *project successful* ***hua hai***. *(Project has become successful because of his excellent communication.)* LCS occurs both inter-sentential and intra-sentential.

LCS occurs in all genres of communication for such speakers, including spoken conversation, email, online chat rooms, blogs and newsgroups. Thus, it seriously impacts attempts to process these exchanges computationally, for the purposes of automatic translation, speech recognition, and information extraction, inter alia (Solorio and Liu, 2008a; Solorio and Liu, 2008b).

With increasing interest in LCS, there is need for large annotated LCS corpora which can support the needs of computational as well as theoretical research. This paper presents one experiment where a corpus of code switched sentences is annotated for identifying code switch points using crowd sourcing methods. The data collection serves as the first attempt at creating a repository for LCS data. Also the annotations of LCS points will shed light into the nature of this phenomenon and will be an initial building block for the development of interesting analytical and predictive models for automatic LCS processing systems. It is widely accepted that LCS actually follows a certain pattern and that it does not occur randomly. Several studies in sociolinguistics and theoretical linguistics have investigated this issue however on a small scale (Poplack, 2001; Myers-Scotton, 1993).

2 Hindi and Hinglish

Hindi is the national language of India and native language of many parts of the country. It has continuously been impacted by varied languages and dialects of the country, the most influential of which is English. English expanded its roots into India from the time Britain occupied the country. It was initially the language of the elite upper class but as the education system became widespread, English spread across the whole country. With the proliferation of scientific advancements in the English speaking world and India's race for technology acquisition, we note that English has almost

Proceedings of the 9th Workshop on Asian Language Resources, pages 36–40,
Chiang Mai, Thailand, November 12 and 13, 2011.

become an Indian language. In fact, Indians from different parts of India who speak mutually unintelligible native Indian languages use English as the bridge language to communicate. The pervasiveness of English coupled with the Hindi education throughout the country led to rapid development of **Hinglish**, a term coined to describe the use of Hindi and English words in the same utterance, Hinglish LCS.[1] Since Hindi is a morphologically rich language, we even often observe LCS occurring on the morphological level. Hinglish has become a widespread phenomenon (as a language in and of itself even) used by Indians in different parts of the world. It is obvious that the context switches from Hindi to English are very frequent and some words that are borrowed such as *Thank You*, *Please*, *Crazy* are almost Hindi words, as they have become part of the Indian native lexicon. One important reason that smooth switch can occur between Hindi and English is that words from any of these languages can fill the lexical gaps in the sentence of the other. It is important to point out that LCS is beyond nonce and borrowing, the phenomenon in Hinglish is that of significant amounts of words and chunks are switched back and forth in the same utterance, it is not a matter of isolated borrowed words that are highly frequent in the Hindi lexicon.

Our paper attempts to describe an initial large scale collection of LCS data and annotate it on the word/token level. Several linguistic studies have investigated Hinglish on a theoretical level (Bhatt, 1997; Joshi, 1985) as well as socio-pragmatic level as in the work of Bhatt and Bolonyai (2008). The studies suggest that LCS occurs in a systematic manner. However to our knowledge no large collection of LCS data for Hinglish exists, let alone detailed annotations for such a collection. Our initial attempt is to fill this gap such that it would be of utility to both the theoretical linguistics as well as the computational processing fields.

3 Corpus Collection

We needed content where the matrix language was Hindi with frequent code switches to English. Modern Hindi novels are rich sources for such content as they use Hinglish frequently. The content of two sites: *www.hindinovels.net* and *www.abhivyakti-hindi.org* were crawled using perl scripts and broken into sentences to develop the corpus. Some Hindi sentences with no CS were mixed with these sentences to prepare an optimal blend of sentences for annotations. The final corpus consisted of 10500 sentences comprising 193285 tokens.

4 Experiment Setup

Amazon Mechanical Turk (AMT) is a marketplace to host surveys where **requesters** host some questions which are answered by **workers**, aka turkers. It has been widely accepted that the use of crowd sourcing techniques for the collection of data annotations is a worthwhile effort (Snow et al., 2008). The benefit of using crowd sourcing lies in a rapid collection cycle, sometimes at the expense of quality. Hence the challenge lies in designing and simplifying the task and presenting it to lay people in generic terms. But also setting performance metrics for accepting such annotations. We carried out our experiments on AMT where we asked the turkers to identify each word in a sentence as one of the following categories:[2]

1. Hindi- *aaya*(came),*gaya*(went),*hum*(we)
2. English- usual English words, for example, *eat, grin, happy*
3. Foreign Proper Name- *John*,*Stella*, *IBM*
4. Indian proper Name- *Ramesh*,*Ganesh*, *Anjali*
5. Unknown- Any word which can not be classified into any of the above categories

The experiment was set up as a survey with three Hinglish sentences on one page. Each of such pages is termed a Human Intelligence Task (HIT) and a collection of HITs is termed a task on AMT. Our collection of 10500 sentences was divided into 7 tasks, each task containing 500 HITs with 3 sentences each. Each word in a sentence had a drop down list containing the above options associated with it, with the default option being Hindi. The AMT turkers then marked each word in the sentence as one of the options above. A minimum of two turkers were allowed to work on a single HIT or the same set of 3 sentences in order to allow overlap for agreements/disagreements on same set of words. Accordingly all the data was at

[1] For the purposes of this paper, we are not interested in the inter sentential LCS.

[2] For this pilot annotation, we did not include the more complex annotation of mixed Hinglish morphology. We decided to postpone that annotation for a later phase.

least doubly annotated.

A subset of HITs (10% of the corpus size) was gold annotated by a native bilingual speaker of Hindi and English. We designed the set up of the HITs such that for any given turker at least one sentence in a HIT overlapped with a gold annotation. Then the turker whose sampled HIT annotations agreed with the gold annotation less than 95% were discarded. Initially, 136 turkers submitted the results, out of which 85 turkers scored above the set 95% threshold. The HITs that were rejected were resubmitted to AMT for re-annotation. With resubmission results, 8 more turkers were added as they scored above the 95% threshold bringing the total number of turkers to 93. Accordingly, the overall data was annotated by 93 turkers, 10% of the overall 10500 sentences is three way annotated with gold annotation and by two turkers.

5 Experiment Results and Statistics

In this section we present detailed results on the collected annotations. We calculate inter-turker agreements based on how many times a turker agreed on a category within the same HIT with the other turkers who co-annotated the same HIT. The results for turkers were then aggregated to find the total number of agreements for each category. The resulting confusion matrix is shown in Table 1. The legend for the table is as follows:

h- Hindi
e- English
f- Foreign Proper Name
i- Indian Proper Name
u- Unknown

Each cell of the confusion matrix corresponds to agreement counts for any turker aggregately with respective co-turkers.

The following detailed statistics show the percentage classification agreement among the co-turkers in different categories for the majority annotated class on the word level. As mentioned above, each HIT was annotated by two turkers. In our detailed statistics, we observe the number of times two turkers agreed on a category label per word in the same HIT. We report below the percentage of aggregate pairwise agreements

	h	**e**	**f**	**i**	**u**
h	167195	1875	370	535	426
e	2546	11800	229	47	215
f	578	253	3996	143	45
i	546	45	120	1467	29
u	442	212	40	32	99

Table 1: Confusion Matrix of the aggregate turkers' annotations for the different categories

among the turkers for those categories. We report the results of the analysis by the majority class. Hence for those instances that are considered Hindi across the HITs, 98.1% of the times, some two turkers agreed on a Hindi label.

All in all, the data had 193285 word instances, corresponding to 14658 word types, 88.16% word instances were considered Hindi by the majority of turkers, 7.67% instances were considered English by the majority of turkers, 2.59% words were considered Foreign Proper names, and 1.14% were considered Indian Proper names, finally 0.42% were considered Unknowns. The following statistics reflect the confusion on the majority label by aggregate pairs of turkers.

For majority class Hindi word instances (88.16% of the word instances):

Hindi- 98.1%
English- 1.1%
Foreign Proper Name- 0.22%
Indian Proper Name- 0.31%
Unknown- 0.25%

Hence, turkers agreed 98.1% of the time that the label for these 88.16% of the word instances are Hindi, however, some set of the turker pairs confused 1.1% of this Hindi data set as English, while 0.25% of the time pairs of turkers considered these Hindi words as Unknown.

For majority class English word instances (7.67% of the word instances):

Hindi- 17.16%
English- 79.53%
Foreign Proper Name- 1.54%
Indian Proper Name- .32%
Unknown- 1.45%

The turkers agreed 79.53% of the time that

the label for these 7.67% of the word instances are English, however, some set of the turker pairs confused 17.16% of this English data set as Hindi, 1.54% as Foreign Proper Name, 0.32% as Indian Proper Name and 1.45% of the time pairs of turkers considered these English words as Unknown

For majority class Foreign Proper Name word instances (2.59% of the word instances):

Hindi- 11.52%
English- 5.04%
Foreign Proper Name- 79.68%
Indian Proper Name- 2.85%
Unknown- .9%

The turkers agreed 79.68% of the time that the label for these 2.59% of the word instances are Foreign Proper Name, however, some set of the turker pairs confused 11.52% of this Foreign Proper Name data set as Hindi, 5.04% as English, 2.85% as Indian Proper Name and 0.9% of the time pairs of turkers considered these Foreign Proper Names as Unknown

For majority class Indian Proper Name word instances (1.14% of the word instances):

Hindi- 24.74%
English- 2.04%
Foreign Proper Name- 5.44%
Indian Proper Name- 66.47%
Unknown- 1.31%

For majority class Unknown word instances (0.42% of the word instances):

Hindi- 53.58%
English- 25.7%
Foreign Proper Name- 4.85%
Indian Proper Name- 3.88%
Unknown- 12%

The above statistics are the aggregated results, we note that the results for each of the 93 turkers taken individually, as compared to their respective co-turkers follow the same trend as the aggregated results. For example, if we compare an individual turker with co-turkers, majority of agreements are Hindi-Hindi, English-English and so on. Similarly, disagreements are also proportionate to above statistics.

A detailed token level analysis also showed similar trends. We analyzed a sample of 1304 tokens of which 1005 have a Hindi root and 245 are of English etymology. 27 tokens were Foreign Proper Names and 26 were Indian Proper Names. The turkers agreed 98.45% times that the tokens are Hindi over the total occurrences of sample Hindi root tokens. They agreed 79.41% times that the token is English over tokens with English root, 75.74% times agreed that the token is Foreign Proper Name for Foreign Proper Name tokens. The turkers agreed 74.58% times that the token is an Indian Proper Name for Indian Proper Name tokens. The turkers were observed to confuse Hindi tokens and Indian Proper Name tokens as 22.63% times, i.e. they mutually agreed that the token is Hindi when it was in fact an Indian Proper Name.

We further analyze the agreement on a complete sentence level, where turkers agreed on the annotation for every token in the sentence, we found only 57 such sentence annotations.

6 Analysis of Results

As depicted by the above statistics, the largest percentage of agreement was for the words marked in the Hindi category. There was about 98% agreement over such words which can be attributed to two reasons. Firstly, Hindi being the matrix language, a dominant part of words in the sentences were Hindi. Secondly, although there were very few instances where the turkers completely agreed on each word of a sentence, they had almost no confusion in identifying the Hindi words in a sentence.

For a word classified as English by a turker, the co-turkers agreed 80% times. However, about 17% co-turkers confused such words as Hindi. An obvious reason for such observation is the fact that some of the English words have blended so well with Hindi that even the native Hindi speakers are not able to recognize them as English words. For example, English words such as **cycle, car, train, plate, bread** have become part of Hindi lexicons and the native speakers unintelligibly consider these words as Hindi itself in their conversations. This shows the seamless mingling of English words in Hindi to such an extent that they are indistinguishable as English words.

There was agreement for majority of Foreign and Indian Proper Names (79.68% and 66.47% respectively). The highest percentage of disagreements were observed when the co-turkers marked proper names as Hindi words. This may be attributed to the fact that capitalization does not exist in the Hindi script for proper names, and they might be misconstrued as other parts of speech. For example, **Pawan** could be a name and could be used as a noun meaning **air** as well. Similarly, **Anant** could be used as a name or an adjective meaning **with out an end**.

The Unknown category showed some interesting results. The agreement over Unknown category was much less among turkers. Instead, majority of co-turkers marked such words as Hindi words (53.58% times). After analysis, it was found that a major reason for this observation was because turkers were confused on morphologically mixed words. For example, plural of **company** after morphological adjustment becomes **companiyon** in Hinglish. A turker was not able to classify such words distinctly since it is half Hindi and half English from his point of view. Moreover, we believe that the fact that we have a default Hindi tag, could have contributed to the confusion. In our next iteration of annotation experiments, we will make sure to avoid a default tag.

If we consider the overall results, more than 90% of agreements were for Hindi words followed by English, Foreign Proper Name, Indian Proper Name and Unknown categories, in that order. This along with results for each of the individual categories shows that the turkers have high confidence while marking the Hindi words. English words, foreign proper names and Indian proper names also show good confidence with agreement over majority of them. Majority of disagreements in different categories were classified as Hindi which shows the tendency of the turkers to mark the word, about which they are confused, as Hindi itself, or simply leave it as default. Based on analysis of results above in conjunction with the interturker and gold agreements, it can be affirmed with high confidence that apart from the *Unknown* category words, the turkers converge on the correct category significantly above chance indicating the feasibility of the approach.

7 Conclusion and Future Directions

In this paper we presented an initial attempt at building a large scale repository of manually annotated LCS data for Hinglish. We believe we have established that crowd sourcing is a good method for inducing such annotations. In the near future we plan on annotating more data. We plan on adding a new category label of mixed morphology. Finally, we intend to perform the same annotation task for other language pairs.

References

Aravind Joshi. 1985. Processing of sentences with intrasential code switching. *Natural Language Parsing: Psychological, Computational and Theoretical Perspectives*. Cambridge University Press, Cambridge, UK.

Carol Myers-Scotton. 1993. Common and Uncommon Ground: Social and Structural Factors in Codeswitching *Language in Society*, 22(4):475–503.

Rakesh M. Bhatt. 1997. Code-switching, constraints, and optimal grammars. *Lingua*, 102(4):223–251.

Rakesh M. Bhatt and Agnes Bolonyai. 2008. Code-switching and optimal grammars . *Proceedings from the Annual Meeting of the Chicago Linguistic Society*, 44(2):109–122.

Rion Snow, Brendan O'Connor, Daniel Jurafsky and Andrew Ng. 2008. Cheap and fast but is it good? evaluating non-expert annotations for natural language tasks. *Proceedings of the EMNLP 2008, Honolulu, Hawaii*, 254–263.

S Poplack. 2001. Code-switching (Linguistic). N. Smelser and P. Baltes (eds.) *International Encyclopedia of the Social and Behavioral Sciences*, 2062–2065.

Thamar Solorio and Yang Liu. 2008. Learning to Predict Code-Switching Points. *Proceedings of the EMNLP 2008, Honolulu, Hawaii*, 973–981.

Thamar Solorio and Yang Liu. 2008. Part-of-Speech Tagging for English-Spanish Code-Switched Text. *Proceedings of the EMNLP 2008, Honolulu, Hawaii*, 1051–1060.

Linguist's Assistant: A Resource For Linguists

Stephen Beale
University of Maryland, Baltimore County
Baltimore, MD
sbeale@cs.umbc.edu

Tod Allman
Onyx, Consulting
Baltimore, MD
todallman@yahoo.com

Abstract

The Linguist's Assistant (LA) is a practical computational paradigm for describing languages. In this paper we describe how to use LA with naturally occurring texts that exemplify interesting target-language linguistic phenomena. We will describe how such texts can be semantically analyzed using a convenient semi-automatic document authoring interface, in effect adding them to LA's standard semantic-based elicitation corpus. We then exemplify the language description process using a phenomenon that is prevalent in our research: alienable vs. inalienable nominal possession.

1 Introduction

The Linguist's Assistant (LA) is a practical computational paradigm for efficiently and thoroughly describing languages. Previously (Beale, submitted) we reported on the first of three main modes of LA-based language description: using the provided elicitation corpus of semantically analyzed sentences as the starting point and organizing principle from which the user describes the linguistic surface forms of a language using LA's visual lexicon and grammatical rule development interface. We described the semantic representation system that we developed and the make-up of the corpus of semantically analyzed texts that are meant to provide examples of a large subset of the kinds of meaning found in written communication. We described the visual lexicon and grammatical rule development interface that the linguist uses to record the lexical and grammatical knowledge needed to translate the semantic corpus into the target language.

Having read this previous paper, a respected linguist offered some valid criticism (valid, that is, if LA were restricted to this first mode of operation): "I am, in general, a bit reluctant to use ready-made questionnaires, for all sorts of reasons -- some of which you mention yourself. It so happens that my personal interest has always been on naturalistic speech… I have always paid a lot of attention to what actually shows up in everyday spoken speech, as opposed to what could exist 'grammatically' but is never heard. I've always wondered why so many grammars or articles in linguistics work on sentences such as '*The man sees the woman.*' which don't appear ever in naturalistic speech." (Alex François, personal communication). This paper is an attempt to counter such criticism by describing the second mode of operation in LA-based language description: acquiring language data and grammatical knowledge using naturally occurring texts that exemplify interesting target-language linguistic phenomena. We will describe how such texts can be semantically analyzed using a convenient semi-automatic document authoring interface, in effect adding them to the standard semantic-based elicitation corpus used in the first mode of operation. We exemplify the process using a linguistic phenomenon that is prevalent in Oceanic languages: alienable vs. inalienable nominal possession. Ishizuka (2010) describes a similar phenomenon in Japanese and Korean.

Before moving on, we should mention the third mode of LA-based language description: acquiring knowledge (lexical and grammatical) to cover pre-authored stories ("authored" in our context means that a semantic representation has been prepared). The semantically motivated elicitations from mode one combined with knowledge gained from the naturally occurring texts of mode two provide a solid foundation for lexicon and grammar development, but we have found that adding to that the experience and discipline of acquiring the knowledge necessary to generate actual story-length texts is invaluable. This is usually the best opportunity for documenting phenomena that is more lexically de-

Proceedings of the 9th Workshop on Asian Language Resources, pages 41–49,
Chiang Mai, Thailand, November 12 and 13, 2011.

pendent since the vocabulary in the semantic-based elicitation stage is quite limited. It also provides a test bed for the knowledge acquired in the first two modes of operation. For this reason we include several pre-authored community development texts/stories with LA. After acquiring the necessary lexical and grammatical knowledge for the target language, a draft translation of the stories can be produced and checked for naturalness and accuracy. LA has been used in this mode to produce a significant amount of high-quality translations in Jula (a Niger-Congo language), Kewa (Papua New Guinea), North Tanna (Vanuatu), Korean and English. Work continues in Vanuatu, with additional languages planned in the near future. We argue that the high quality results achieved in these translations demonstrate the quality and coverage of the underlying language description that LA produces. Beale et al. (2005) and Allman and Beale (2004; 2006) give more information on using LA in translation and for documentation on the evaluations of the translations produced.

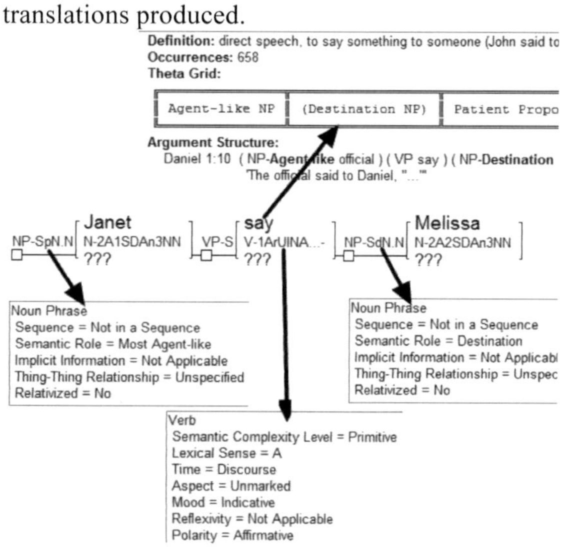

Figure 1: Semantic representation

LA is available for academic research and non-profit applications. Tutorials and related papers are also available, although a significant portion of our planned work is to produce better tutorials and workshop materials. The developers plan to offer tutorials at various conferences in the near future. We emphasize that LA is a work in progress. In any practical product with complex theoretical underpinnings there is a development loop where a "critical mass" of theory is implemented, the surrounding support tools created and tested, the product is used and evaluated, and then work begins again on improving the theoretical base. LA is somewhere in the late stages of the "being used and evaluated" step of this cycle. We certainly intend to improve the theoretical basis of each aspect of the product as time goes on, in large part as a result of the feedback, suggestions and criticisms of our users.

2 Introduction to LA

Consult Beale (submitted) for details on LA, including the semantic representation language and the visual lexicon and grammar interfaces. In order to make this paper self-contained, we summarize some of this material here.

A top-level view of the semantic representation is shown in Figure 1. Each concept "bundle" takes up three lines of text (for example, in the middle of the figure, "say", the line directly below that with "V-1ArUINA", and the line with the question marks). The top line is the English gloss of the concept. It must be emphasized that the English gloss is only shown for convenience; it represents a concept in our ontology. The upper yellow box appears upon a mouse-over of the concept; it provides details about the definition and usage of the concept. The middle line of the concept bundle consists of letters and numbers that specify the semantic features associated with this particular instance of the concept. These features can be viewed by placing the cursor over the concept. Note that phrases and clauses have semantic features defined for them in the same way that instances of concepts do. As shown in the figure, noun phrases have features such as semantic role. Verbs have time, aspect and mood features. Nouns have features that specify person, number and various reference-related meanings. The bottom line of the concept bundle is the "translation" of the concept into whatever target language is currently loaded (in the figure, question marks are displayed because no language is loaded). This "translation" is only a mapping to a target root word; often a concept will require more than a direct word-for-concept substitution.

Each sentence in the elicitation corpus has a semantic representation. In the first mode of language description described in Beale (submitted), the linguist needs to "teach" the computer how to realize each of the parts of that input semantic representation, including all the individual concepts, each of the semantic features and all the relationships (such as the case role relationships, discourse relations and adposition relationships). Backing up a bit, it is important to think about the overall nature of an LA project. The elicitation corpus contains the wide range of phenomena that we are interested in documenting. The linguist creates the lexical knowledge and grammatical rules so that LA's built-in text generator can accurately translate the underlying meaning of the included semantic-based elicitation corpus. After this first stage is complete, the second stage of language description that is highlighted in this paper begins: using naturally occurring target language texts to describe important linguistic phenomena that occur in the language. Once the descriptive phases are complete, the resulting computational model of the language can be used in translation applications or output as part of a language documentation project.

	Stems	Glosses	type
1	aprend	learn	-er
2	habl	speak	-ar
3	ten	have	-er
4	viv	live	-ir

Figure 2: Lexical features for Spanish

	Stems	Glosses	infinitive	present indic 1st sing
1	aprend	learn	aprender	aprendo
2	habl	speak	hablar	hablo
3	ten	have	tener	tengo
4	viv	live	vivir	vivo

present indic 2nd sing	present indic 3rd sing	present indic 1st pl	present indic 3rd pl
aprendes	aprende	aprendemos	aprenden
hablas	habla	hablamos	hablan
tienes	tiene	tenemos	tienen
vives	vive	vivimos	viven

Figure 3: Lexical forms for Spanish

How does the linguist "teach the computer how to realize"? LA provides a rich, visual interface for building target lexicons and grammatical rules. Figure 2 shows the interface for creating and displaying lexical features, for example, the inflection type (-ar, -er or –ir) of a Spanish verb. Figure 3 shows the interface for displaying forms. Lexical form generation rules can be written to automatically generate each of the forms of a word. The white boxes in Figure 3 are irregular forms that were corrected by the user.

Grammatical rules typically describe how a given semantic structure is realized in the language. The whole gamut of linguistic phenomena is covered, from morphological alternations to case frame specifications to phrase structure ordering to lexical collocations – and many others. Figures 4-8 are examples of various types of grammatical rules. Figure 4 shows a morphophonemic rule; Figure 5 a phrase structure ordering rule; Figure 6 a feature copying rule (as would be used, for example, in Subject-Verb agreement in English), Figure 7 a table, and Figure 8 a theta-grid (or case-frame) realization rule. There are also rules similar to Figure 8 for converting the base semantic representation to a deep structure that is more appropriate for the target language. For example, Kewa[1] has a rule that converts the basic semantics for "X respects Y" into "X lifts-up the name of Y."

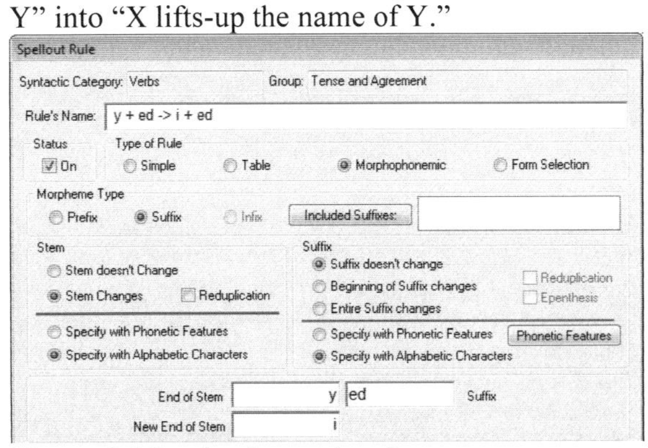

Figure 4: Morphophonemic rule

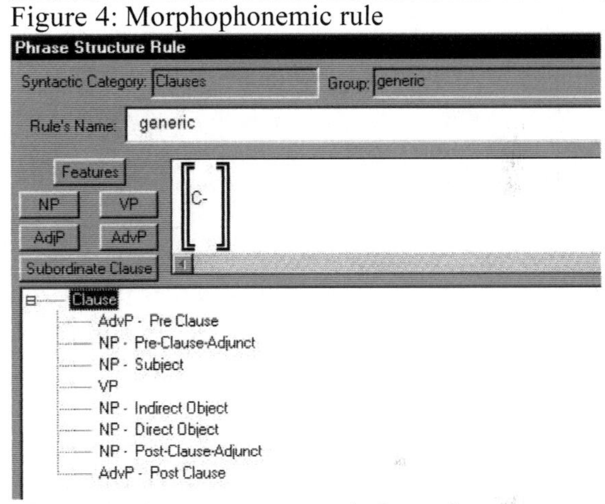

Figure 5: Phrase structure ordering rule

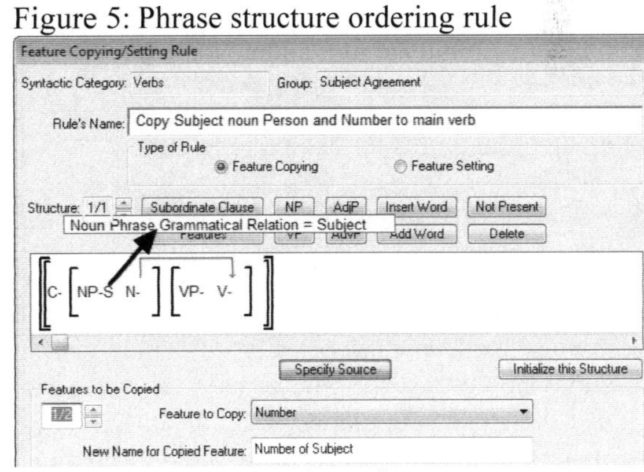

Figure 6: Feature copying rule

Currently, the linguist is responsible for the creation of rules, albeit with a natural, visual interface that often is able to set up the requisite input semantic structures automatically. We continue work on modules that will allow the semi-

[1] Dr. Karl Franklin supplied the Kewa data.

automatic generation of rules similar to research in the BOAS (McShane et al., 2002), LinGO (Bender et al., 2010), PAWS (Black and Black, 2009) and Avenue (Probst et al., 2003) projects. Such modules will, we believe, make LA accessible to a larger pool of linguists. We also provide a growing list of rule templates that linguists can use to describe common phenomena.

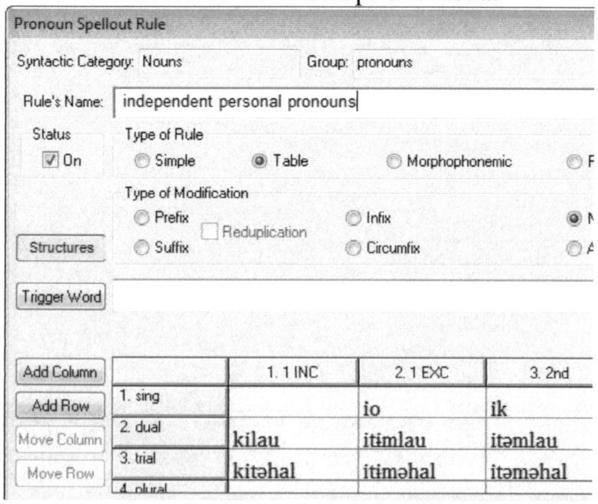

Figure 7: Table rule

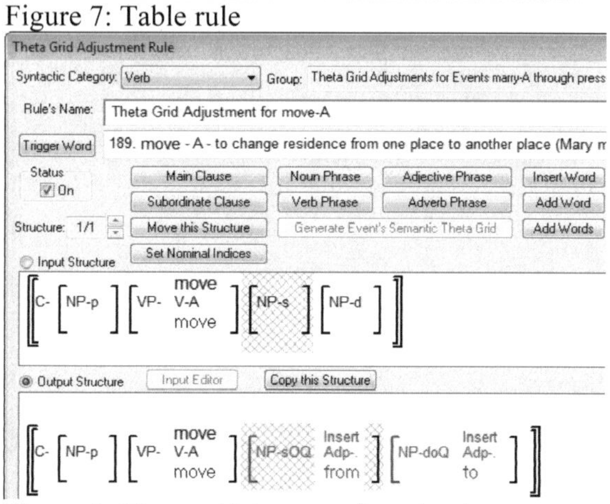

Figure 8: Theta grid (or case-frame) rule

3 Possession in Maskelynes

This paper focuses on using LA to describe a particular linguistic phenomenon using naturally occurring texts. We use alienable vs. inalienable nominal possession in Maskelynes as our case study. Ishizuka (2010) describes a similar phenomenon in Japanese and Korean. Maskeleynes is an Oceanic language spoken by about 1400 people in central Vanuatu. The language data and analysis presented here was inspired by a draft version of David Healey's doctoral thesis (which he has asked me not to directly reference in its present form). In addition to the draft nature of that document, some of the data presented below was extrapolated from the examples without confirmation by a native speaker. As such, we do not intend this to be a linguistic specification. However, the phenomenon described is typical of Oceanic languages and has been directly observed by the author in other Vanuatu languages. For the workshop presentation we will augment or replace this example with one more directly relevant to Asia; the point here is to describe the scope and methodology of LA as a linguistic resource.

Oceanic linguists have historically divided nouns into alienable and inalienable classes.[2] Inalienable nouns always appear with their "possessor." For example, body parts ("my arm") and relatives ("John's father") must occur with their possessor, as just illustrated. Healey also reports the more recently understood distinction of direct vs. indirect possession (Lichtenberk, 1985), which occurs in addition to the alienable vs. inalienable distinction. Directly possessed nouns in Maskelynes carry the marker of possession on the head noun whereas indirectly possessed nouns carry the possessive marker on the possessor noun or pronoun. We summarize the data in the rest of this section and in Figure 9.

In Maskelynes, inalienable nouns (section 1 of Figure 9) can either be directly possessed or indirectly possessed, depending on the class of the noun. Kinship terms and visible body parts generally are directly possessed (section 1A). Directly possessed inalienable nouns take an obligatory possession suffix. If the possessor must be specified (beyond the pro reference of the possession suffix), the possessor noun follows the head noun with no additional marking.

Maskelynes also has indirectly possessed inalienable nouns (section 1B). Some inanimate nouns that must be referred to with a possessor (for example, "his song" and "the home's shadow") and many internal body parts are indirectly possessed. These all follow the 'h' class of indirectly possessed nouns described below.

All alienable nouns (section 2) are indirectly possessed.

All indirectly possessed nouns (sections 1B, 2A and 2B) are either in the 'h' class (section 2A, typically foods and drinks) or the 's' class (section 2B, general nouns). Indirect possession can be realized with a possessive pronoun (that agrees with the 'h' or 's' class, as appropriate), or, when the possessor cannot be a pronoun, a genitive proclitic (hX- or sX- depending on the noun class) attached to the possessor noun, in

[2] See (Ishizuka 2010) for a treatment of alienable vs. inalienable possession in Japanese and Korean.

which case the nominaliser (which generally occurs on nouns) of the possessor is deleted.

1. Inalienable
  A. Directly possessed
    i. Human
      Pro-suffix possessor: *a-na-gw*
        NOM-mother-POSS.1st.excl.sing
        "my mother"
      Possessor must be specified: *a-na-n a-vanuan*
        NOM-mother-POSS.3rd.sing NOM-man
        "the man's mother"
    ii. Non-human
      Pro-suffix possessor: *nX-rie-gw*
        NOM-leg-POSS.1st.excl.sing
        "my leg"
      Possessor must be specified: *nX-rie-n a-vanuan*
        NOM-leg-POSS.3rd.sing NOM-man
        "the man's leg"
  B. Indirectly possessed
    Pronomial possessor: *nX-bwe hagw*
      NOM-song POSSPRO.1st.excl.sing
      "my song"
    Possessor must be specified: *nX-bwe hX-vanuan*
      NOM-song POSS.1st.excl.sing-man
      "the man's song"
2. Alienable (and indirectly possessed)
  A. h class
    Pronomial possessor: *nX-buai hagw*
      NOM-pig POSSPRO.1st.excl.sing
      "my pig"
    Possessor must be specified: *nX-buai hX-vanuan*
      NOM-pig POSS.1st.excl.sing-man
      "the man's pig"
  B. s class
    Pronomial possessor: *nX-kuvkuv sagw*
      NOM-axe POSSPRO.1st.excl.sing
      "my axe"
    Possessor must be specified: *nX-kuvkuv sX-vanuan*
      NOM-axe POSS.1st.excl.sing-man
      "the man's axe"

Figure 9: Possession Examples for Maskelynes

A final noun class relevant to our discussion involves the nominaliser: the human vs. non-human class. Nouns in the human class take the 'a-' nominaliser (section 1Ai) whereas non-human nouns (section 1Aii) take the 'nX-' nominaliser. The 'X' in this nominaliser and in the proclitic is phonologically conditioned; we will leave it as 'X' to simplify the discussion.

The examples in Figure 9 give an exhaustive reckoning of the different realization possibilities (other than the fact that different persons and numbers can be used for the pronouns and possessive suffixes).

4 Describing Possession Using LA

4.1 Authoring Examples

The first step in describing a new phenomenon in LA is to author examples. This process will produce semantically analyzed examples that will be used in the knowledge acquisition stage (sections 4.2 through 4.4 below) and in the testing stage (section 4.5).

Upon starting the document author, the system will ask for input sentences in a controlled English.[3] This is a key benefit and a limitation at the same time. LA is not able to parse target texts into the semantic representation that is needed in the subsequent stages (since it does not have a complete target grammar at this stage). Therefore we allow the user to mentally translate the meaning of the target language examples into the restricted English. Our built-in English analyzer will then semi-automatically produce the semantic analysis with only a small amount of editing of the results required from the user. Of course it would be optimal if the user could enter the examples in the target language and have an automatic semantic analysis performed, but this is impossible in the absence of a target language analyzer. Work has begun, however, on tools that will allow computer-assisted semantic analysis of target texts, which would obviate the need for the user entering simplified English translations.

To describe possession in Maskelynes, the user first enters the restricted English translations of the target sentences from Figure 9, as shown in Figure 10. In practice, because the authoring stage is relatively simple, the user could enter many more examples than shown, including an exhaustive accounting of all the possible combinations of number and person of both the head and possessor nouns. Figure 11 shows (in admittedly small print) a version of the results of the built-in semantic analysis. In the case of the first input phrase "My(John's) mother", the analysis is correct and no further editing is required. Notice that the analyzer chose the correct number and person (1st singular) for "John" and the correct Kinship relationship. For "my leg" the analyzer correctly chose the Body-Part relationship. We continue to work on the

[3] See Beale et. al (2005) for a description of the controlled English and for a description of the authoring process.

accuracy of the built-in English analyzer, but minor adjustments are sometimes necessary.

4.2 Setting Up Target Language Features

The key to describing possession in LA for Maskelynes - and indeed the key to using LA in general - is to first identify and create the target language features that will make it easy to write surface rules. In the case of possession, we need to know what class of noun is involved: inalienable vs. alienable, direct vs. indirect, and human vs. non-human. The user can define these features in the LA lexicon and specify the correct value for each for each noun root. Figure 12 shows an example lexicon for Maskelynes' nouns. Note the "class" and "human?" features.

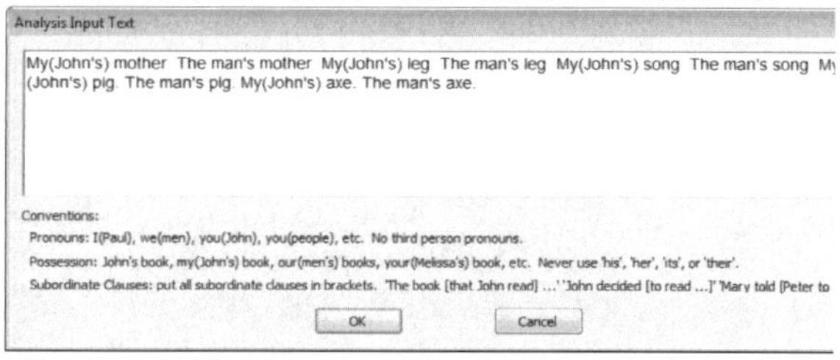

Figure 10: Document authoring input text

As you can see in Figure 9, it is also necessary to know whether the possessor noun is specified or whether there can be a suffix or a full pronoun reference to it. A key step in describing possession is to define such a feature on nouns, "Realization Type," which takes the values "noun" or "pronoun." The user can delay consideration of how to actually set that feature for later. To conserve space we do not show the trivial process of defining a new target feature.

Some words in Figure 9 have a POSS suffix (like *a-na-gw* in 1Ai). Some words have a gentive proclitic (like *hX-vanuan* in 2A). And other words have no possession affixes (like *nX-bwe* in 2A). Therefore another target feature that will make the final surface production rules easier is the "Noun Possession Type" feature for nouns. This will take the values "none", "possessed" and "genitive proclitic". This is the key feature used in our discussion in section 4.3 below. Again, the assignment of the correct value to this feature can be assumed when writing the rule that generates the actual surface form (section 4.3); later (section 4.4) the rule(s) will be written to set the correct value.

Note the difference between lexical features that are associated with a given root (and are defined in the lexicon) and the general target features that are defined outside the lexicon and whose values must be set by some rule. Given the two general features ("Realization Type" and "Noun Possession Type") and the two lexical features (class and human?), it will be possible to construct surface rules that implement the full range of possible realizations of possession.

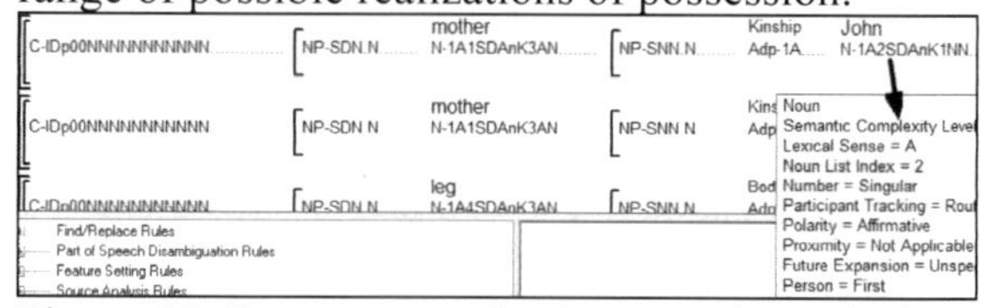

Figure 11: Document author's semantic analysis

Syntactic Category: Nouns | Setup | Stems | Features

	Stems	Glosses	Class	human?
1	buai	pig	Food & Drink alienable	no
2	bwe	song	General indirect inalienable	no
3	dan	spleen	Food & Drink indirect inalienab	no
4	kuvkuv	axe	General alienable	no
5	na	mother	Kin direct inalienable	yes
6	natu	child	Kin direct inalienable	yes
7	rie	leg	General direct inalienable	no
8	siloh	plate	Food & Drink alienable	no
9	soa	spouse	Kin direct inalienable	yes
10	tabx	grandparent	Kin direct inalienable	yes
11	tahoh	lung	Food & Drink indirect inalienab	no

Figure 12: Maskelynes noun classes in lexicon

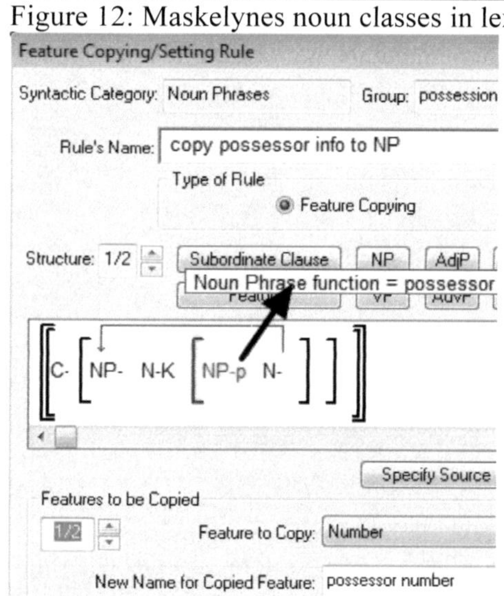

Figure 13: Feature copying rule

The preparation of features needed by the surface rules often has a final source: feature copying rules. In this case, the surface rules for choosing the correct possessor suffix to add to the main root for directly possessed nouns (section 1 of Figure 9) must have access to the person and number of the possessor. Figure 13 shows a rule that copies the number of the embedded possessor to the NP level of the main phrase. Note that the resulting feature will be called "possessor number." A similar rule copies the person. Figure 13 also shows (in the mouse-over tooltip pointed to by the arrow) an additional Noun Phrase target feature not mentioned yet: the "Noun Phrase Function." This feature can have various values in Maskelynes, but will be set to the value "possessor" for these examples by a rule that we will not discuss (which is, in fact, the main point: we can define these features and use them without worrying about the rules that will correctly set their values). The fact that we did not mention (or even think of!) this feature earlier points out what must be obvious: the need for target features often only becomes evident as you consider how to build an easy surface rule, or even as you think about how to write the rules to set other target features (in section 4.4 below). In all, there are three sources of features to be used in the surface rules: lexical features, target features defined by the user and set by rules, and features that were copied from other constituents using feature copying rules.

4.3 Writing Surface Rules

Space prevents us from presenting all of the surface rules; we concentrate on the rule that produces the possessive suffix for directly possessed nouns (section 1 of Figure 9). Figure 14 shows the surface table rule that adds possessive suffixes to directly possessed nouns. The three arrows point to mouse-over pop-ups that detail which feature values are referenced in the indicated row or column. The top-left corner cell of the table is a catch-all cell; the input must match this corner cell or the rule will not apply. In this case, the requirement is that the "Noun Possession Type" feature of the noun must be "possessed." The "Noun Possession Type" is the target feature we discussed above. Later, we will need to write a rule to set its value to "possessed" for directly possessed head nouns. But the main point here is that this particular surface rule that adds the suffixes is extremely simple if we assume the presence of that feature. The pop-up that appears on a mouse-over of the first row shows that this row refers to the "possessor person" feature on the Noun Phrase. This feature (which is a copy of the person of the possessor noun) was created above using the feature copying rules. Likewise the first column refers to the "possessor number" feature on the Noun Phrase, also copied using the feature copying rule described above. The table rule simply defines the correct suffixes for each combination of Person and Number.

A rule of similar complexity will add the genitive proclitic (as for *hX-vanuan*) for the case when the Noun Possession Type feature is "genitive proclitic." A separate rule will add the possession word (for example, *hagw or sagw)* when the Possession Type is "none." In general, we have identified the three major realization cases, created a target feature to reflect these choices, and then wrote three different surface output rules to actually realize each choice. Each rule is relatively simple (once a proficiency in using LA is attained). At this stage we have not even worried about the rules that set the target feature that makes these surface output rules possible.

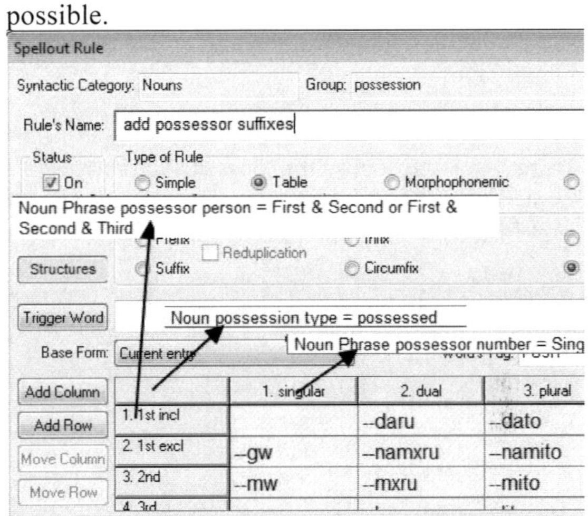

Figure 14: Table rule for possessive suffixes

4.4 Writing Rules that Set Target Features

The surface rules described above are simple because a well thought-out system of target features is assumed. The target features can come from the lexicon, from user-defined target features, or from feature copying rules. Those that are user-defined need to have their values set with rules. The "Noun Possession Type" feature is set by rules (Figures 15-18) that examine the class of noun and the realization type (pronoun or full noun) of the possessor.[4]

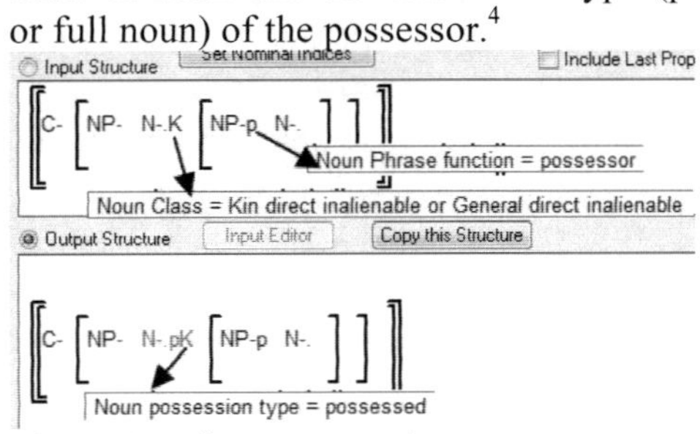

Figure 15: direct possession

Figure 15 corresponds to the directly possessed case in 1A of Figure 9. Note the "Noun

[4] For the workshop presentation, we will go over the Noun Possession Type rules in greater depth and/or use a completely different example related to Asian linguistics.

Possession Type" is attached to the head noun. Figures 16 and 17 correspond to the indirectly possessed cases in Figure 9 in which possessive suffixes are used; note that the output feature is attached to the possessor noun. And finally Figure 18 corresponds to the indirect case where a genitive proclitic is used.

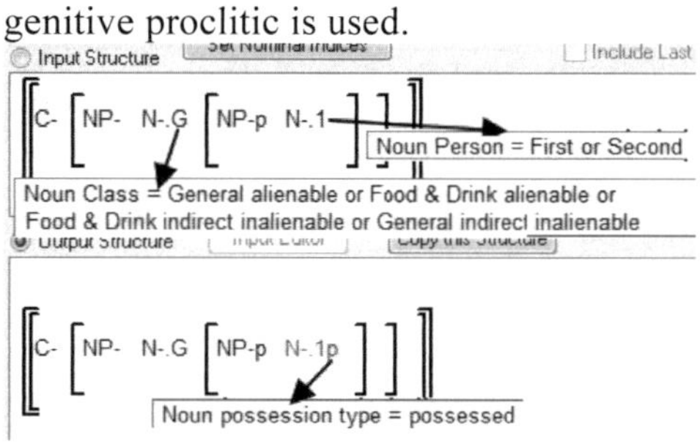

Figure 16: Indirect with possessive suffix on possessor (1st or 2nd person possessor)

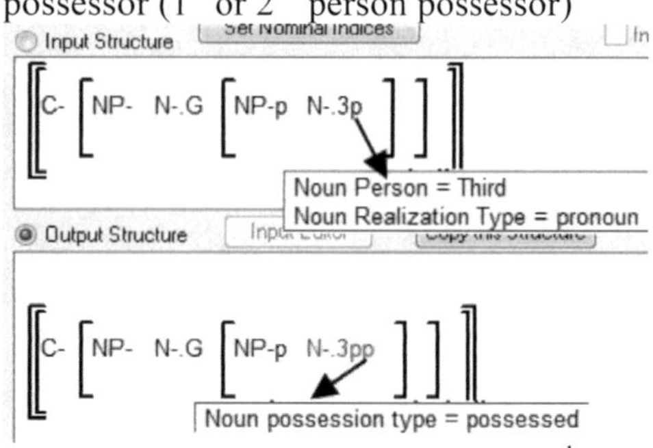

Figure 17: Similar to Figure 17 for 3rd pronoun

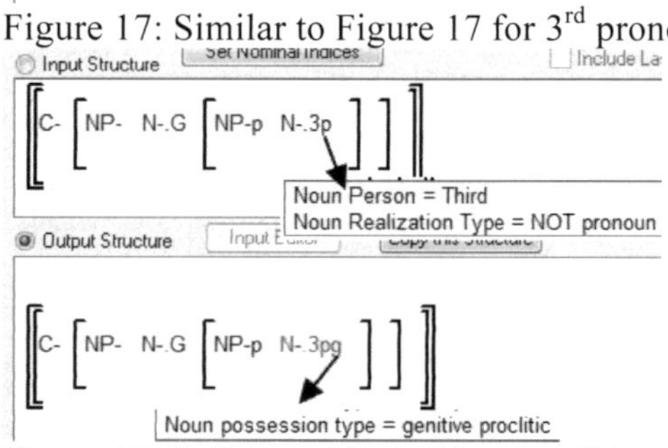

Figure 18: Indirect with genitive proclitic

We will not pretend that these rules are easy to follow in a paper with such limited space. We will be able to describe the rules better at the presentation. The main point is that the rules themselves are relatively simple to construct once a certain level of familiarity with LA is attained. The progression we presented here is typical. The surface rules (section 4.3) are easy because we assume the presence of well thought-out target features. The rules that set these target features (section 4.4) can be simple as well. Thus the entire process is often straightforward once the methodology is learned. The workshop presentation will focus on using LA to implement this methodology.

4.5 Testing the Acquired Knowledge

The final stage of knowledge acquisition is to test the system by generating target text from the example sentences that were previously authored (section 4.1). Figure 19 shows the results of generating from the authored examples. The top text box contains the target translations, which in this case match the expectations from Figure 9. The yellowish mouse-over pop-up that appears when the cursor is placed on *a-na-gw* shows all of the rules that were applied that were related to that target word. LA also includes a breakpoint mechanism that allows the user to step through the application of a rule. These debugging tools (Allman, 2010) are invaluable in the knowledge acquisition, test, revision loop that is typical.

Conclusion

This paper along with Beale (submitted; 2011) describe the two main modes of language description in LA: 1) using the provided semantic elicitation corpus to guide knowledge acquisition, and 2) using naturally occurring texts that exemplify interesting target-language linguistic phenomena. We demonstrated the latter process in this paper using possession in Maskelynes as an example. In future publications we intend to present other linguistic phenomena, summaries of LA's overall use to document a specific language, and further tutorials and descriptions of LA itself.

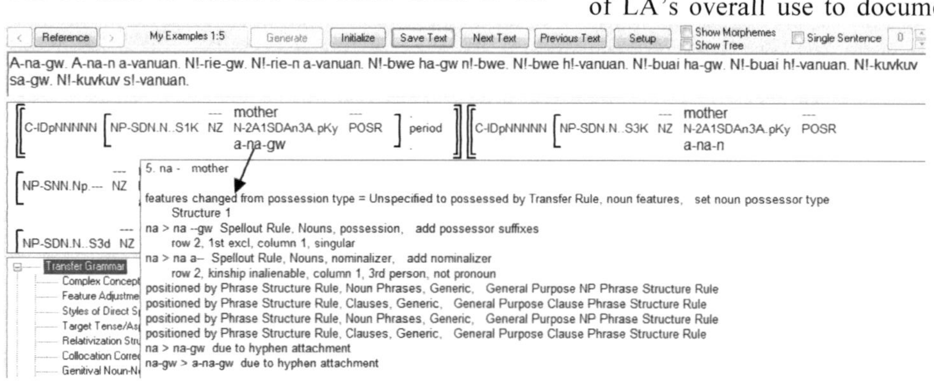

Figure 19: Output translations

References

Tod Allman. 2010. The Translator's assistant: a multi-lingual natural language generator based on linguistic universals, typologies, and primitives. Arlington, TX: University of Texas dissertation.

Tod Allman and Stephen Beale. 2006. "A natural language generator for minority languages," in Proceedings of SALTMIL, Genoa, Italy.

Tod Allman and Stephen Beale. 2004. "An environment for quick ramp-up multi-lingual authoring," International Journal of Translation 16(1).

Stephen Beale. Submitted. "Documenting endangered languages with linguist's assistant." Language Documentation and Conservation Journal. Draft available at: http://ilit.umbc.edu/sbeale/LA/papers/DEL-for-LDC-journal.pdf

Stephen Beale. 2011. Using Linguist's Assistant for language description and translation. In Proceedings of The 5th International Joint Conference on Natural Language Processing (IJCNLP-11) Demonstrations, Chiang Mai, Thailand.

Stephen Beale, S. Nirenburg, M. McShane, and Tod Allman. 2005. "Document authoring the Bible for minority language translation," in Proceedings of MT-Summit, Phuket, Thailand.

Emily Bender, S. Drellishak, A. Fokkens, M. Goodman, D. Mills, L. Poulson, and S. Saleem. 2010. "Grammar prototyping and testing with the LinGO grammar matrix customization system," in Proceedings of the ACL 2010 System Demonstrations.

Sheryl Black and Andrew Black. 2009. "PAWS: parser and writer for syntax: drafting syntactic grammars in the third wave," http://www.sil.org/silepubs/PUBS/51432/SILForum2009-002.pdf.

Tomoko Ishizuka. 2010. Alienable-Inalienable asymmetry in Japanese and Korean possession. *University of Pennsylvania Working Papers in Linguistics*. Volume 16: issue 1.

Frantisek Licthenberk. 1985. "Possessive constructions in Oceanic languages and Proto-Oceanic," in Austronesean linguistics at the 15th Pacific Science Congress, Canberra: Pacific Linguistics C-88.

Marjorie McShane, Sergei Nirenburg, Jim Cowie, and Ron Zacharski. 2002. "Embedding knowledge elicitation and MT systems within a single architecture," Machine Translation 17(4), pp.271-305.

Katharina Probst, Lori Levin, Erik Petersen, Alon Lavie and Jaime Carbonell. 2003. "MT for minority languages using elicitation-based learning of syntactic transfer rules," Machine Translation 17(4), pp.245-270.

Multi-stage Annotation using Pattern-based and Statistical-based Techniques for Automatic Thai Annotated Corpus Construction

Nattapong Tongtep and Thanaruk Theeramunkong
School of Information, Computer, and Communication Technology,
Sirindhorn International Institute of Technology, Thammasat University, Thailand
131 Moo 5, Tiwanont Rd., Bangkadi, Muang, Pathum Thani, Thailand 12000
{nattapong,thanaruk}@siit.tu.ac.th

Abstract

An automated or semi-automated annotation is a practical solution towards large-scale corpus construction. However, special characteristics of Thai language, such as lack of word-boundary and sentence-boundary markers trigger several issues in automatic corpus annotation. This paper presents a multi-stage annotation framework, containing two stages of chunking and three stages of tagging. Two chunking stages are named entity extraction by pattern matching and word segmentation by dictionary; and three following tagging stages are dictionary-based, pattern-based and statistical-based tagging. Applying heuristics of ambiguity priority, entity extraction is performed first on an original text using a set of patterns, ordered by pattern ambiguity. Later segmenting a sequence of characters into words, the chunks are tagged according to the order of ambiguity, using dictionary, pattern and statistics. Focusing on the reduction of human intervention in corpus construction, our experimental results show that the pattern-based tagging was able to reduce the number of tokens marked as unknown by the dictionary-based tagging by 44.76% and the statistical-based tagging was able to reduce the number of terms identified as ambiguous by both above methods by 72.44%. The proposed multi-stage framework reduced the number of tokens requiring human annotation (those that are tagged unknown or with multiple tags) to 16.35% of the entire corpus.

1 Introduction

As fundamental tasks, word segmentation, part-of-speech (PoS) tagging, and named entity (NE) recognition are essential steps for various natural language processing applications such as text summarization, machine translation, and question answering. For languages like Burmese, Khmer, Lao, Tamil, Telugu, Bali, and Thai, which have no distinct boundary marker between words and sentences (similar to space and a full stop in English), word segmentation is required. PoS tagging is another important task which assigns some syntactic categories such as verb, noun, and preposition to a token or a word for resolving innate ambiguities, while more specific predefined categories, such as person name, location, and organization are assigned in the steps of NE recognition (NER). The current trend in PoS tagging and NE recognition is to utilize machine learning techniques, which are trainable and adjustable. Several supervised learning techniques were successfully attempted and have shown reasonable performances. For PoS tagging, Pandian and Geetha (2009) utilized conditional random fields (CRFs), a probabilistic model, to segment and label sequence data, to tag and chunk PoS in Tamil. Huang et al. (2009) showed that a bigram PoS tagger using latent annotations could achieve the accuracy of 94.78% when testing on a set of the Penn Chinese Treebank 6.0. For NE recognition, Lee et al. (2004) presented a two-level Korean named entity classification (NEC) by cascading highly precise lexical patterns and the decision list. Park and Rim (2008) classified bio-entities by using predicate-argument structures as the external context features. Tongtep and Theeramunkong (2010) investigated a method to segment Thai word and recognize named entity simultaneously by using the concept of character clusters together with discriminative probabilistic models. Such machine learning tasks, however, require high quality tagged corpora or annotated corpora for training which are costly and time consuming to construct. Only few research works studied the methods to build the an-

Proceedings of the 9th Workshop on Asian Language Resources, pages 50–58,
Chiang Mai, Thailand, November 12 and 13, 2011.

notated corpus with less human effort. Lee et al. (2010) proposed rules to judge the tagging reliability for constructing a Korean PoS tagged corpus. Since the quality of the PoS annotation in a corpus is crucial for the development of PoS taggers, Loftsson (2009) examined three error detection methods for automatically detecting hand-correct PoS errors in the corpus. For a corpus size, Sasano et al. (2010) reported that the performance was not saturated even with a corpus size of 100 billion Japanese words when analyzing case frame acquisition for predicate-argument structure. In Thai, Isahara et al. (2000) constructed a PoS tagged corpus named ORCHID manually. The ORCHID corpus was annotated on three levels: paragraph, sentence, and word. Charoenporn et al. (2006) constructed another lexicon by using existing machine-readable dictionaries, and a sort of semantic constraint called selectional preference is added into the lexicon by analyzing Thai texts on the web. Lately, Theeramunkong et al. (2010) proposed a framework and annotation tools for tagging named entity and constructing corpus in Thai. With their annotation tools, the Thai-NEST corpus was annotated and verified by collaborative experts. However, the process is very costly and time consuming. Until now, there have been no research reports on minimizing human intervention in automatic construction of either Thai PoS or named entity tagged corpus.

In this paper, we propose a multi-stage annotation framework to construct a PoS- and NE-tagged corpus with word segmentation for Thai language with less human effort. First, a list of words and named entities is acquired from online resources. Later, they are used in the two succeeding chunking processes to extract named entities and segment words. Three automatic tagging processes are applied together with designed lexical and context features. In the dictionary-based tagging level, ambiguous tokens, unambiguous tokens, and unknown tokens are discovered. In the next step, the number of unknown tokens is reduced by the pattern-based tagging. Finally, the number of ambiguous tokens is decreased in the statistical-based tagging level. The remaining part of this paper is organized as follows. In Sect. 2, the writing system in Thai is discussed. The overall system architecture is proposed in Sect. 3. In Sect. 4, experimental settings and results are reported. The experimental results are discussed in Sect. 5. Finally, a conclusion is illustrated in Sect. 6.

2 Thai Writing System

An example of Thai texts is depicted as shown in Fig. 1. The Thai language consists of 44 consonants, 21 vowel symbols, 4 tone markers for its 5 tonal levels, and a number of punctuation marks. Thai writing system is left-to-right direction, without spaces between words and no uppercase and lowercase characters. Vowels can be written before, after, above, or below consonants, while all tone marks, and diacritics are written above and below the main character.

A Thai word is typically formed by the combination of one or more consonants, one vowel, one tone mark, and one or more final consonants to make one syllable. Thai verbs are not inflected for any of tense, gender, and singular or plural form. Instead, we put some additional words to express their inflection. Moreover, Thai has no distinct boundary maker between words and sentences, like space and a full stop in English.

3 The Framework

In this paper, we propose a multi-stage annotation framework to construct high-quality annotated corpora with less human effort. The framework comprises two stages for chunking and three stages for tagging (see Fig. 2). Two stages for entity chunking are (1) entity extraction and (2) word segmentation. Three stages for entity tagging are (1) dictionary-based tagging level, (2) pattern-based tagging level, and (3) statistical-based tagging level. Entities are named entities, parts-of-speech and other entities such as punctuation and number. A list of entities and a list of words are reusability resources for developing a tagged corpus. In the step of entity extraction, unsegmented tokens and segmented tokens are extracted from the input texts using a set of patterns, ordered by pattern ambiguity, then unsegmented tokens are segmented by the longest matching technique in the step of word segmentation. Segmented tokens are tagged by three-stage entity tagging. Start with the dictionary-based tagging level, ambiguous tokens, unambiguous tokens, and unknown tokens are discovered. The number of unknown tokens is reduced in the pattern-based tagging level. In the statistical-based tagging level, the number of ambiguous tokens is decreased. Instead of check-

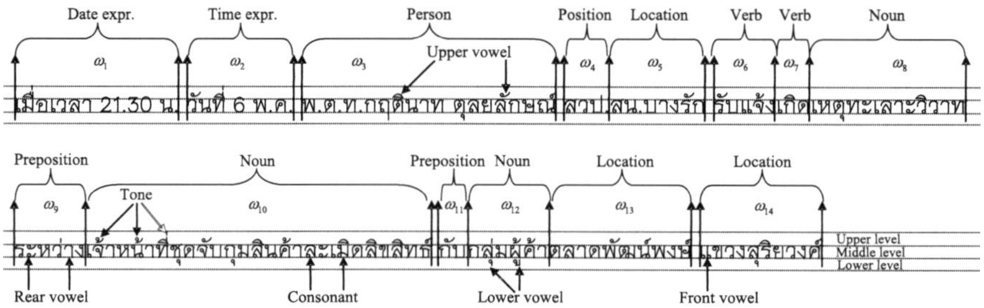

Figure 1: An example of Thai texts

ing all tags in the corpus which is costly and time consuming, our framework can minimize human interposition by indicating which tokens are ambiguous or unknown. Each stage for chunking and tagging is explained in the next section.

3.1 Entity Chunking

For entity chunking, two stages are (1) entity extraction and (2) word segmentation. In this step, a list of words and a list of entities are gathered from online resources such as Thai Wikipedia[1], The Royal Institute[2], The Government Information System[3], Company in Thailand[4], Longdo Dict[5], and YAiTRON[6].

3.1.1 Entity Extraction

In Algorithm 1, we collected the list of entities as entity seeds from online resources. In this step, the list of entities are location (LOC), person name (PER), position (POS), family relationship (FAM), date (DAT), time expressions (TIME) and some parts-of-speech which are longer than two syllables i.e., adverb (ADV), conjunction (CONJ), question phrase (QUE), and verb (VERB). Entity seeds are applied to extract segmented and unsegmented tokens from the input texts. A segmented token is a token which appears in the entity seeds while an unsegmented token is a token which disappears in the entity seeds. Segmented tokens are used to extract left and right contexts, and construct patterns using inner clues and contexts. An inner clue is a set of hint texts which is an apart of named entity. For example, *Her Royal Highness Princess Maha Chakri Sirindhorn* is a person name appears in the person seeds, *Her Royal Highness Princess* will be an inner clue. Generally, one entity may have several entity tags such as "Washington" (person and location). In this paper, constructing patterns using inner clues and contexts will solve the ambiguity in entity tags.

Unsegmented tokens such as named entities outside the list of entity seeds, will be detected and segmented by entity patterns. Segmented tokens or extracted entities from this step will be verified and added to the existing list of entities by experts. This work, the entity extraction is performed before the word segmentation and PoS tagging, since entities in the Thai language are formed by the combination of two or more words, and likely to be transliterated words and unknown words. The remaining unsegmented tokens will be segmented in the word segmentation process.

3.1.2 Word Segmentation

Words are basic components in the language processing. Detecting words in an inherent-vowel alphabetic language that does not have explicit word boundary is highly difficult. To segment words with a good performance and minimizing human interposition for constructing tagged corpus, pattern matching techniques are applied by using a suitable list of words or dictionaries as a tool. It is known that the word segmentation performance will decrease when the processed text contains words that not existing in the dictionary (e.g., unregistered words or unknown words or misspelling words). In order to simply discover unknown word, the longest matching is utilized. Dictionaries or list of words are gathered from online resources, and applied to segment the remaining unsegmented tokens from the prior entity extraction process using the longest matching technique. In this paper, we exploit the longest matching technique implemented by Haruechaiyasak (2006) and

[1] http://th.wikipedia.org
[2] http://www.royin.go.th
[3] http://www.oic.go.th/ginfo
[4] http://www.companyinthailand.com
[5] http://dict.longdo.com
[6] http://th.lug.wikia.com/wiki/YAiTRON_(English-Thai_dictionary)

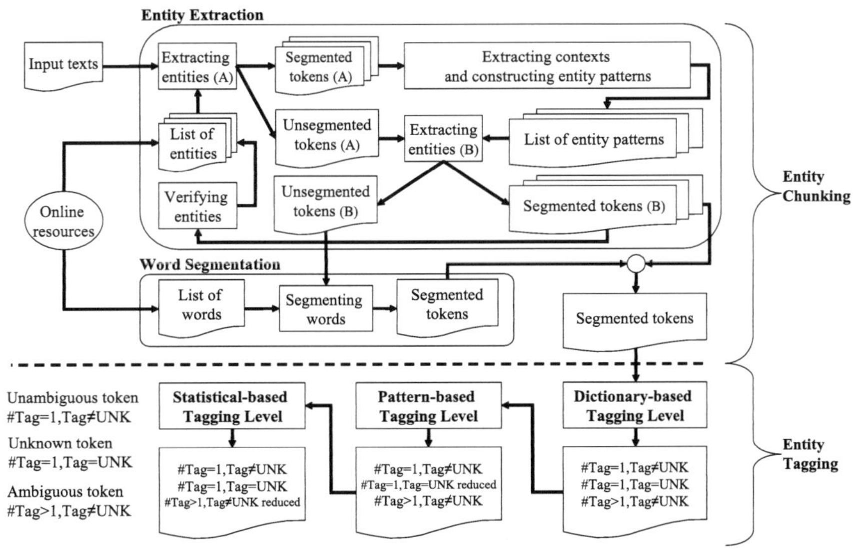

Figure 2: The framework of multi-stage annotation for automatic Thai annotated corpus construction

use our collected list of words. The output from the entity extraction and the word segmentation, i.e., segmented tokens, will be used as the input data in the dictionary-based tagging level which is one of entity tagging stages.

3.2 Entity Tagging

The entity tagging process consists of 3 tagging levels; (1) dictionary-based tagging level, (2) pattern-based tagging level, and (3) statistical-based tagging level. In this work, 25 entity types i.e., 13 parts-of-speech, 6 named entities, and 6 other entities, are defined for constructing tagged corpus as shown in Table 1. "UNK" is one of entity types which is used to assign tokens that do not belong to 24 predefined entity types.

Figure 3 illustrates an example of the transformation of tags among three tagging levels in the entity tagging process. Three entity tagging stages are described in the next section.

3.2.1 Dictionary-based Tagging Level

In this level, unknown tokens, ambiguous tokens and unambiguous tokens are detected.

An unknown token is a string which does not belong to 24 predefined entity types. This token will be assigned by "UNK" entity tag ($\#Tag = 1, Tag =$ UNK).

An unambiguous token is a string which belongs to one of existing entity types, except "UNK" ($\#Tag = 1, Tag \neq$ UNK).

An ambiguous token is a string which has more than one possible parts-of-speech in the dictionary. ($\#Tag > 1, Tag \neq$ UNK). A set of entity tags assigned to each ambiguous token is called "multi-entity" tag.

For example, w X;UNK means a token w is assigned a single entity tag as unknown (UNK) since the token does not belong to predefined 24 entity types. x X;NOUN means a token x is assigned a single entity tag as noun (NOUN) only. y X;CLAS;NOUN means a token y is possible to have an entity tag as classifier (CLAS) or noun (NOUN). A set of entity tags i.e., CLAS;NOUN, is a "two-entity" tag. z X;CONJ;NOUN;PREP means a token z is possible to have an entity tag as conjunction (CONJ), noun (NOUN), or preposition (PREP). A set of entity tags, i.e., CONJ;NOUN;PREP, is a "three-entity" tag. "X;" is a separator among a token and a set of entity tags, and ";" is a separator among entity tags.

In this paper, the YAiTRON[7] dictionary is exploited to assign the entity tags. YAiTRON: Yet Another (Lex)iTRON is a Thai-English and English-Thai dictionary data, stored in a well-formed XML format. YAiTRON is a homogeneous structure dictionary, adapted from National Electronics and Computer Technology Center (NECTEC[8])'s LEXiTRON[9] dictionary. YAiTRON covers 32,350 unique words

[7]http://th.lug.wikia.com/wiki/YAiTRON_(English-Thai_dictionary)
[8]http://www.nectec.or.th
[9]http://lexitron.nectec.or.th

Dictionary-based Tagging Level	Pattern-based Tagging Level	Statistical-based Tagging Level
กระทรวงพาณิชย์ X;NOUN	กระทรวงพาณิชย์ X;NOUN	กระทรวงพาณิชย์ X;NOUN
กับ X;CONJ;NOUN;PREP	กับ X;CONJ;NOUN;PREP	กับ X;CONJ;NOUN;PREP
กลุ่ม X;CLAS;NOUN	กลุ่ม X;CLAS;NOUN →	กลุ่ม X;NOUN
ผู้ค้า X;UNK →	ผู้ค้า X;POS	ผู้ค้า X;POS
ตลาด X;NOUN	ตลาด X;NOUN	ตลาด X;NOUN
พัฒน์ X;UNK	พัฒน์ X;UNK	พัฒน์ X;UNK
พง X;NOUN	พง X;NOUN	พง X;NOUN
ษ์ X;UNK	ษ์ X;UNK	ษ์ X;UNK
<SPACE> X;SPC	<SPACE> X;SPC	<SPACE> X;SPC
แขวงสุริยวงศ์ X;LOC	แขวงสุริยวงศ์ X;LOC	แขวงสุริยวงศ์ X;LOC
และ X;CONJ	และ X;CONJ	และ X;CONJ

Figure 3: An example of tag transformation in entity tagging

with 13 parts-of-speech i.e., adjective (ADJ), adverb (ADV), auxiliary verb (AUX), classifier (CLAS), conjunction (CONJ), determiner (DET), end (END), interjection (INT), noun (NOUN), preposition (PREP), pronoun (PRON), question phrase (QUE), and verb (VERB).

3.2.2 Pattern-based Tagging Level

There are some tokens that always have only one PoS when beginning with some specific texts. For example, every token begins with "Ministry of" always be a location, or every token begins with "Minister of" always be a person's position. We assemble such texts by observing prefix's tokens from the dictionary. So far we have had 125 patterns with 100% correctness; 1 pattern for adverb, 49 patterns for locations, 61 patterns for nouns, 11 patterns for positions and 3 patterns for verbs. An example of Thai grammatical patterns is shown in Fig. 4. Furthermore, other tokens such as comment, number, punctuation, space, and English characters, will be automatically assigned with an entity tag as COMMENT, NUM, PUNC, SPC and ENG, respectively. Every unknown token which does not match with these patterns in this tagging level will be assigned with an entity tag as UNK.

Entity	#Patterns	Example
Adverb	1	อย่าง-
Location	49	กระทรวง-, สถานี-, ชมรม-, ธนาคาร-, อุทยาน-,...
Noun	61	เครื่อง-, หนังสือ-, กระเป๋า-, กล้อง-, โครงการ-,...
Position	11	นัก-, ผู้-, รัฐมนตรี-,...
Verb	3	ตัด-, ร้อง-, ไม่-

Figure 4: An example of Thai grammatical patterns

3.2.3 Statistical-based Tagging Level

In this level, only ambiguous tokens will be transformed to unambiguous tokens. Since an ambiguous token comprises more than one possible parts-of-speech which specified in the dictionary, we need a PoS classifier to select the best PoS tag among them. In machine learning tasks, several PoS classifiers were trained from the large PoS tagged corpora which are costly and time consuming to construct. In this work, we exploit naïve Bayes classifier since it only requires a small amount of training data to estimate the parameters necessary for classification. A naïve Bayes classifier is a simple probabilistic classifier based on applying Bayes' theorem with strong (naive) independence assumptions. In spite of their naive design and apparently over-simplified assumptions, naïve Bayes classifier has worked quite well in many complex real-world situations. In this paper, nine context features are defined as shown in Table 2.

Predicting an entity tag t given a vector of context features $F = (f_1, f_2, ..., f_{|F|})$. One simple way to accomplish this is to assume that once the entity tag is known, all the features are independent. The result is based on a joint probability model of the form:

$$p(t|F) = p(t_j) \prod_{i=1}^{|F|} p(f_i|t_j). \quad (1)$$

The best entity tag t_{best} among the output tags T is

Algorithm 1: Entity extraction

Input : texts
Output: segmented tokens sTB and unsegmented tokens uTB

Extracting entities (A):
- Collect list of entities e from online resources, ordered by longest matching
- Label e in the input texts
  $\rightarrow$ segmented tokens (A) sTA
  $\rightarrow$ unsegmented tokens (A) uTA

Extracting contexts and constructing entity patterns:
- Extract contexts surround sTA
  $\rightarrow$ 20 characters from sTA's left $cL20$
  $\rightarrow$ 20 characters from sTA's right $cR20$
- Collect inner clue entities from e
  $\rightarrow$ list of inner clues $iClue$
- Construct patterns for e
  $\rightarrow$ pattern $p = \{cL20\}\{uTA \in iClue$ and $uTA \ni cL20, cR20\}\{cR20\}$

Extracting entities (B):
- Label p in uTA
  $\rightarrow$ segmented tokens (B) sTB
  $\rightarrow$ unsegmented tokens (B) uTB

Verifying entities:
- Verify sTB
- Add the correct sTB to e

$$t_{best} = \arg\max_{t_j \in T} p(t_j) \prod_{i=1}^{|F|} p(f_i|t_j). \qquad (2)$$

We train our statistical-based entity tagger by using the traditional naïve Bayes classifier. Since an ambiguous token will be transformed to an unambiguous token if the best single entity tag obtained from its multi-entity tag, we modify Equation 2 to support our constraint. The best entity tag t'_{best} among a multi-entity tag $T' = (t'_1, t'_2, ..., t'_n)$ is

$$t'_{best} = \arg\max_{t'_j \in T'} p(t'_j) \prod_{i=1}^{|F|} p(f_i|t'_j), \qquad (3)$$

$$t'_{best} = \begin{cases} t'_{best} & \text{if } t'_{best} \in T' \\ T' & \text{otherwise} \end{cases}$$

Type	Entity	Description
PoS	ADJ	Adjective
	ADV	Adverb
	AUX	Auxiliary verb
	CLAS	Classifier
	CONJ	Conjunction
	DET	Determiner
	END	End
	INT	Interjection
	NOUN	Noun
	PREP	Preposition
	PRON	Pronoun
	QUE	Question phrase
	VERB	Verb
NE	DAT	Date expr.
	FAM	Family rlat.
	LOC	Location
	PER	Person
	POS	Position
	TIM	Time expr.
Other	COMMENT	Comment
	ENG	English
	NUM	Number
	PUNC	Punctuation
	SPC	Space
	UNK	Unknown

Table 1: The list of possible entity tags

4 Experimental Settings and Results

We collected 764 Thai news documents comprised 1,559,330 characters from the web. In the step of entity extraction, we acquired 19,528 segmented tokens as shown in Table 3. In the step of word segmentation, a list of 155,088 unique words acquired from online resources were applied to segment unsegmented tokens. Using the longest matching technique, we obtained 316,653 segmented tokens. By entity chunking i.e., 336,181 tokens were used as the input data for the entity tagging process.

Table 4 shows the experimental results from the entity tagging process. Unambiguous tokens, unknown tokens, and ambiguous tokens were classified in the dictionary-based tagging level, while the pattern-based tagging level and the statistical-based tagging level reduced the number of unknown tokens and the number of ambiguous tokens, respectively. In the dictionary-based tagging level, 24.14% and 10.94% of all token texts were tagged as unknown tokens and ambiguous tokens. The number of unknown tokens reduction in the pattern-based tagging level is 44.76% (reduced from 81,170 unknown tokens in the dictionary-based tagging level to 44,841 unknown tokens in the pattern-based tagging level). The number of

Token Type	Dictionary-based	Pattern-based	Statistical-based
$\#Tag = 1, Tag \neq$ UNK (Unambiguous tokens)	218,237 (64.92%)	254,566 (75.72%)	281,205 (83.65%)
$\#Tag = 1, Tag =$ UNK (Unknown tokens)	81,170 (24.14%)	44,841 (13.34%)	44,841 (13.34%)
$\#Tag > 1, Tag \neq$ UNK (Ambiguous tokens)	36,774 (10.94%)	36,774 (10.94%)	10,135 (3.01%)
Total tokens	336,181 (100.00%)	336,181 (100.00%)	336,181 (100.00%)

Table 4: The experimental results of the entity tagging

Feature	Definition
tagL2	The second left entity tag
tagL1	The first left entity tag
tagR1	The first right entity tag
tagR2	The second right entity tag
tagL2L1	Two entity tags from left
tagR1R2	Two entity tags from right
tagL2L1R1	Two entity tags from left and one entity tag from right
tagL1R1R2	One entity tag from left and two entity tags from right
tagL2L1R1R2	Two entity tags from left and right

Table 2: Features for the statistical-based tagging level in the entity tagging process

Entity	#Tokens
Adverb	1,342
Conjunction	658
Date	1,386
Family relationship	99
Location	3,781
Person	5,010
Position	467
Question phrase	6
Time	2,571
Verb	4,208
TOTAL	19,528

Table 3: The statistical results of the entity extraction

unknown tokens in the dictionary-based tagging level transformed to unambiguous tokens in the pattern-based tagging level is described in Table 5.

Moreover, in the pattern-based tagging level, 13.34% of all tokens were tagged as unknown tokens. The number of ambiguous tokens reduction in the statistical-based tagging level is 72.44% (reduced from 36,774 ambiguous tokens in the pattern-based tagging level to 10,135 ambiguous tokens in the statistical-based tagging level). In the statistical-based tagging level, 3.01% of all token texts were tagged as ambiguous tokens and 13.34% of all token texts were tagged as unknown tokens. Our entity tagging process can increase the

UnK → UnA	#Tokens
UNK → UNK	44,841
UNK → COMMENT	14,331
UNK → NUM	6,867
UNK → PUNC	4,350
UNK → NOUN	3,386
UNK → POS	2,738
UNK → VERB	1,947
UNK → SPC	1,058
UNK → LOC	956
UNK → ADV	447
UNK → ENG	249
TOTAL	81,170

Table 5: The statistical results of the tag transformation from unknown tokens in the dictionary-based tagging level to unambiguous tokens in the pattern-based tagging level (UnK → UnA)

number of unambiguous tokens up to 83.65%. In this experiment, there were 34 multi-entity tags; 20 two-entity tags, 12 three-entity tags; 1 four-entity tag and, 1 five-entity tag. There are some tokens or words that can be classified as classifier (CLAS), noun (NOUN), preposition (PREP), or pronoun (PRON) depending on contexts. The maximum number of possible tags for a token is set to 5 that is CLAS;CONJ;NOUN;PREP;VERB. NOUN;VERB is a two-entity tag which is highly occurred in the pattern-based tagging level as an ambiguous token, followed by CLAS;NOUN. All ambiguous tokens with their two-entity tag i.e., INT;NOUN can be transformed to unambiguous tokens. Among three-entity tags, ADJ;ADV;AUX is highly occurred in the pattern-based tagging level, followed by NOUN;PREP;VERB. More than 80% of tokens with one of the following 11 multi-entity tags can be transformed to unambiguous tokens by using the proposed context features together with the additional constraint of the joint probability model in the statistical-based tagging level.

- Two-entity tag: INT;NOUN, CLAS;VERB,

PREP;VERB, CONJ;VERB, NOUN;VERB

- Three-entity tag: CLAS;INT;NOUN, NOUN;PREP;VERB, CLAS;NOUN;VERB, CLAS;NOUN;PRON, DET;NOUN;VERB
- Five-entity tag: CLAS;CONJ;NOUN;PREP;VERB

5 Discussion

In this section, the experimental results are discussed. The accuracy of each process was independently verified. This applies to each of the steps including the dictionary-based tagging.

In the entity extraction, we can successfully tag parts-of-speech for tokens longer than two syllables (i.e., adverb, conjunction, question phrase and verb) and named entities (i.e., date, family relationship, location, position and time) with 100% correctness. For tagging person name, we achieved up to 91.95% correctness. Due to the fact that Thai language has no word boundary, extracting entities may not be straightforward. For example, a string whose spelling is equivalent to a short verbal word in a dictionary may not be such a verbal word but just a part of a longer string which indicates another word. From this point of view, it seems better to focus on only a longer verb phrase. Then one potential constraint is to handle a verb phrase that is longer than two syllables. This constraint also handles adverb, conjunction and question phrase that are longer than two syllables. Furthermore, named entities i.e., date, family relationship, location, position and time have explicit boundary, except person name.

In the word segmentation process, the correctness decrease when the processed text contains words that do not exist in the dictionary or list of words. Longest matching algorithm can be considered as using some heuristics to solve the ambiguity problem by selecting the longest possible term. From the experimental results, we obtained 13.34% unknown tokens.

In the dictionary-based tagging level, the performance depends on the reliability of the dictionary. In this work, a token was assigned with possible parts-of-speech defined in well-known dictionaries. From this assumption, all unambiguous tokens, unknown tokens and ambiguous tokens were correctly classified.

In the pattern-based tagging level, our patterns can transform 36,329 unknown tokens to be unambiguous tokens with 100% correctness (from 81,170 unknown tokens in the dictionary-based tagging level to 44,841 unknown tokens in the pattern-based tagging level). Among 44,841 unknown tokens from this level could be unknown words or misspelling words or unregistered word in the dictionary. To solve these problems, human effort is required.

In the statistical-based tagging level, 26,639 ambiguous tokens were transformed to be unambiguous tokens in this level (from 36,774 ambiguous tokens in the pattern-based tagging level to 10,135 ambiguous tokens in the statistical-based tagging level). The accuracy of this tagger is relatively high since it selects the best entity tag for ambiguous tokens from theirs possible tags. If the best entity tag can not obtain from its possible tags, ambiguous tokens will not be transformed to unambiguous tokens.

We conclude that the dictionary-based tagging level and the pattern-based tagging level achieved 100% correctness. Based on statistics, the statistical-based tagging level can help to reduce unambiguous tokens. The performance of the entity chunking stage, especially the word segmentation process, affects the overall performance of the entity tagging stage. Anyway, our multi-stage annotation framework helps to minimize the manual effort in constructing a Thai entity annotated corpus. The expert can focus on selecting the correct PoS from all possible parts-of-speech provided by the dictionary for ambiguous tokens and correct unknown tokens, that is only 16.35% to complete the annotated corpus construction (3.01% from ambiguous tokens and 13.34% from unknown tokens). However, there might be errors even in unambiguous tokens since the correctness of entity extraction, the correctness of word segmentation, and the accuracy of the statistical-based tagger are not 100%. In order to construct an annotated corpus where all annotations are correct, human experts should check not only unknown and ambiguous tokens but also unambiguous tokens. Since the accuracies of the automatically determined word segments and tags are high enough, the proposed system would alleviate human burden even when experts should check all tokens.

6 Conclusion and Future Work

This paper has presented a multi-stage annotation framework to minimize the manual effort in constructing a Thai entity annotated corpus. We propose a new tagging strategy that can automatically detect and reduce unknown tokens and ambiguous tokens. Even a small decrease in the amount of manual annotation task can achieve significant cost savings in constructing a large-scale entity annotated corpus. The proposed framework can provide a new and convenient way to construct annotated corpora, control the quality of the corpus, and reduce the amount of manual annotation. As future work, we plan to create new rules to detect more new content entities among various domains. The measurement of the tagger's reliability and developing an annotation verification system are also investigated.

Acknowledgments

This work has been supported by the Thailand Research Fund (TRF), under Grant No. BRG50800013, a TRF Royal Golden Jubilee Ph.D. Program, under Grant No. PHD/0034/2550, the National Electronics and Computer Technology Center, Thailand, under Grant No. NT-B-22-KE-38-54-01, Government Research Fund via Thammasat University, Thailand, and the National Research University Project of Thailand Office of Higher Education Commission.

References

Thatsanee Charoenporn, Canasai Kruengkrai, Thanaruk Theeramunkong, and Virach Sornlertlamvanich. 2006. Construction of thai lexicon from existing dictionaries and texts on the web. *IEICE - Trans. Inf. Syst.*, E89-D:2286–2293, July.

Choochart Haruechaiyasak. 2006. Longlexto: Tokenizing thai texts using longest matching approach.

Zhongqiang Huang, Vladimir Eidelman, and Mary Harper. 2009. Improving a simple bigram hmm part-of-speech tagger by latent annotation and self-training. In *NAACL '09: Proceedings of Human Language Technologies: The 2009 Annual Conference of the North American Chapter of the Association for Computational Linguistics, Companion Volume: Short Papers*, pages 213–216, Morristown, NJ, USA. Association for Computational Linguistics.

Hitoshi Isahara, Qing Ma, Virach Sornlertlamvanich, and Naoto Takahashi. 2000. Orchid: building linguistic resources in thai. *Lit. Linguist Computing*, 15(4):465–478.

Seungwoo Lee, Joohui An, Byung-Kwan Kwak, and Gary Geunbae Lee. 2004. Learning korean named entity by bootstrapping with web resources. *IEICE - Trans. Inf. Syst.*, 87(12):2872–2882, December.

D.-G. Lee, G. Hong, S. K. Lee, and H.-C. Rim. 2010. Minimizing Human Intervention for Constructing Korean Part-of-Speech Tagged Corpus. *IEICE - Trans. Inf. Syst.*, 93:2336–2338.

Hrafn Loftsson. 2009. Correcting a pos-tagged corpus using three complementary methods. In *EACL '09: Proceedings of the 12th Conference of the European Chapter of the Association for Computational Linguistics*, pages 523–531, Morristown, NJ, USA. Association for Computational Linguistics.

S. Lakshmana Pandian and T. V. Geetha. 2009. Crf models for tamil part of speech tagging and chunking. In *ICCPOL '09: Proceedings of the 22nd International Conference on Computer Processing of Oriental Languages. Language Technology for the Knowledge-based Economy*, pages 11–22, Berlin, Heidelberg. Springer-Verlag.

Kyung-Mi Park and Hae-Chang Rim. 2008. Semantic classification of bio-entities incorporating predicate-argument features. *IEICE - Trans. Inf. Syst.*, E91-D(4):1211–1214.

R. Sasano, D. Kawahara, and S. Kurohashi. 2010. The Effect of Corpus Size on Case Frame Acquisition for Predicate-Argument Structure Analysis. *IEICE - Trans. Inf. Syst.*, 93:1361–1368.

Thanaruk Theeramunkong, Monthika Boriboon, Choochart Haruechaiyasak, Nichnan Kittiphattanabawon, Krit Kosawat, Chutamanee Onsuwan, Issariyapol Siriwat, Thawatchai Suwanapong, and Nattapong Tongtep. 2010. THAI-NEST: A Framework for Thai Named Entity Tagging Specification and Tools. In *CILC '10: Proceedings of the 2nd Int'l Conference on Corpus Linguistics (CILC10), May 13-15, 2010*, pages 895–908, May.

Nattapong Tongtep and Thanaruk Theeramunkong. 2010. Simultaneous character-cluster-based word segmentation and named entity recognition in thai language. In *Proceedings of the Fifth International Conference on Knowledge, Information and Creativity Support Systems (KICSS 2010), November 25-27, 2010*, pages 167–175.

Philippine Languages Online Corpora: Status, issues, and prospects

Shirley Dita
Department of English and Applied Linguistics, De La Salle University, Manila
shirley.dita@gmail.com

Rachel Edita O. Roxas
Center for Human Language Technologies, College of Computer Studies, De La Salle University, Manila
rachel.roxas@delasalle.ph

Abstract

This paper presents the work being done so far on the building of online corpus for Philippine languages. As for the status, the Philippine Languages Online Corpora (PLOC) now boasts a 250,000-word written corpus of the eight major languages in the archipelago. Some of the issues confronting the corpus building and future directions for this project are likewise discussed in this paper.

1 Introduction

The 171 living Philippine languages have been the subject of linguistic investigations and descriptions all over the world (see Liao 2006; Quakenbush 2005; Reid 1981; *inter alia*). As there are controversial and interesting features of Philippine-type languages that are distinct from other Austronesian languages, Philippinists have focused on the different features of Philippine languages over the years. For instance, Brainard (1994) has looked at voice and ergativity; or the focus system (see Barlaan 1986); or case system (see Ramos 1997); and recently, Dita (2010) on pronominal system. But even with a considerable overlap in syntax and morphology, there is a wide range of typological variety found among the more than one hundred Philippine languages (Reid & Liao 2004). And since the plethora of research in Philippine linguistics has been done by non-Filipinos and/or non-Philippine residents, authors have utilized various means to get hold of data on Philippine languages. The methodological approaches of previous studies on language description can be summed up to three: 1) researchers come to the Philippines and stay in the place where the language is spoken for a time; 2) researchers work with a native speaker of the language who currently resides abroad (close to the researchers); and 3) researchers use printed or published materials about the language of interest. It is against this scenario that building a corpus of Philippine languages was conceptualized.

In Dita, Roxas, & Inventado (2009), the design and scope of the first phase of the corpus building were described. As was mentioned, the primary consideration of the data collection was the comparability of the texts in the languages included. Hence, the first phase of the project included a rather limited text type and category, that is, only written texts with two categories: literary and religious. Although there was a plan then to include journalistic and academic texts, it has been observed that not all languages have these text types.

In what follows, we will describe the second phase of the Philippine Languages Online Corpora (henceforth, PLOC), and its current status in terms of data collection and analysis, its distinguishing features, and the issues encountered in the corpus building. Recommendations and future prospects are then outlined towards the end of the paper.

2 Architecture and Parameters

The initial idea was to pattern PLOC after the International Corpus of English where every variety includes a one million-word collection of both written and spoken texts. And as Dita et al. (2009) have emphasized, the first phase of the project faced serious time constraints. This led to the decision to include the most popular kind of text in any Philippine language: religious and literary texts.

2.1 Size and Scope

The standing goal of the project is to provide a comparable corpus of as many Philippine lan-

Proceedings of the 9th Workshop on Asian Language Resources, pages 59–62,
Chiang Mai, Thailand, November 12 and 13, 2011.

guages as possible. To be able to do this, the first phase of the project consisted of the four top languages of the Philippines (Tagalog, Cebuano, Ilocano, and Hiligaynon) and the Filipino Sign Language (FSL). The second phase includes the next four top languages (Bikol, Kapampangan, Pangasinense, and Waray-waray). Hence, the project now consists of the eight major languages in the Philippines and the FSL.

Language	Native Speakers (Millions)	Percentage of Population
Tagalog	17	24.0
Cebuano	15	21.0
Ilocano	8	11.0
Hiligaynon (3 dialects)	7	10.0
Bicolano (5 dialects)	3.5	7.0
Waray-waray	2.4	4.6
Kapampangan	1.9	3.7
Pangasinan	1.1	2.3
Maguindanao (2 dialects)	1	1.7
Total	56.9	87

Table 1. The major Philippine languages

Initially, there was a plan to pattern the PLOC after the structure and design of the International Corpus of English (ICE) project. As reported by Bautista (2004), the Philippine component of the International Corpus of English (ICE-PHI) which is composed of over one million words (1,106,778 words, to be exact) of spoken and written English, is the first mega-word electronic corpus produced in the Philippines. The PLOC is envisioned to be the first multi-million-word electronic and online corpora of Philippine languages. But as there are more languages included in the project, the 1 million size was reduced to 250,000 words for each language, and the written and spoken was reduced to written only.

To date, PLOC only has the written genre and has two types of writing so far: religious and literary. Hence, for each language included, there are 100,000 words of religious texts and another 150,000 literary texts. Although the limitation of the data poses drawbacks, it is the comparability of the data that was taken into account.

2.2 Some Issues

The collection of texts had its own share of challenges. Even with the advancement of technology or the availability of OCRs, the kind of texts needed for the corpora could hardly be scanned. Religious and literary texts are usually the oldest existing literature on any given language. Some of these texts had to be manually encoded, proofread, verified by a native speaker, tagged for corpus use, then uploaded. In most cases, a particular language has more literary text than religious while in some cases, there are more religious than literary. It is in this case that texts need to be carefully chosen to avoid corpus disproportion.

One of the inevitable limitations of the corpora is the issue of representativeness. As earlier mentioned, the scope of texts for PLOC only includes religious and literary which is very specific. Although a corpus, as Leech (1991) puts it, is ideally a representative of the language variety it is supposed to represent, the PLOC do not claim any representativeness of the languages included. But even with this limitation, the corpora still promise to be reliable bases for any linguistic investigation or analysis of Philippine languages.

2.3 Corpus Tagging

After the data is encoded, verified, and proofread, the next stage is the corpus tagging. In cases where the data exhibit some formatting styles such as texts in boldface, italics, or underline, the codes <b></b>, <i></i>, <u></u> are placed before and after the texts which are boldfaced, italicized, and underlined, respectively. For special characters, the following are used: <pd></pd> for non-end of sentence and <lbl></lbl> for special labels such as bible verses. As far as the data is concerned, these tags are sufficient to cover the special formatting styles and characters found in the documents.

3 Corpus Processing and Tools

3.1 Online Repository

One distinguishing feature of PLOC is its being accessible online, unlike most corpora where they are distributed separately. The data repository is called *Palito,* a Tagalog term which literally means 'stick'. The online repository requires a username and password which can be requested from the website master(s) upon verification of identity. Users can either upload or download a document, both subject to the approval of the webmaster. For users who want to contribute to the existing corpus, they send in their documents, the webmaster verifies accuracy and genuineness of the data then uploads them to the online repository. The repository automatically indexes the documents so they can easily be tracked. *Palito* can be accessed through the following link: ccs.dlsu.edu.ph:8086/Palito

Figure 1. Screenshot of Palito's front page

3.2 Features of Palito

Another feature of the repository is its internal browser. For users who want to search for a particular document, such as short story or song, users are to click the 'document' icon then type in the specific name of the document. All files under this category or name are then displayed.

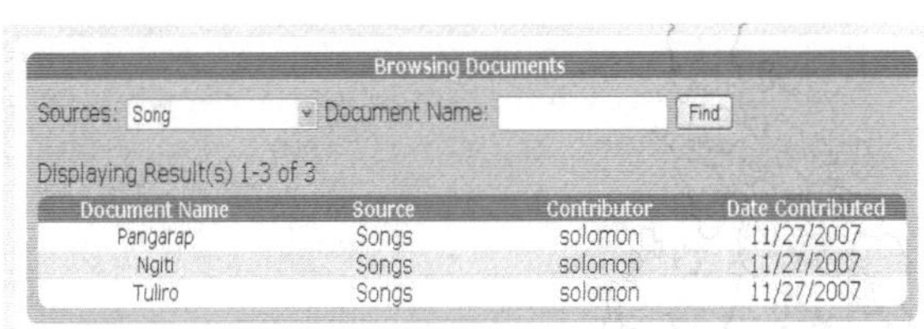

Document Name	Source	Contributor	Date Contributed
Pangarap	Songs	solomon	11/27/2007
Ngiti	Songs	solomon	11/27/2007
Tuliro	Songs	solomon	11/27/2007

Figure 2. *Palito*'s internal browser

For the word frequency feature, the search key is simply typed in the 'filter words'. After which, the results are displayed which makes it more convenient for users who are interested in the distribution of a particular lexical item across the documents. As can be seen in figure 3, the results display the results in descending order, from the files with the most number of the keyword to the least.

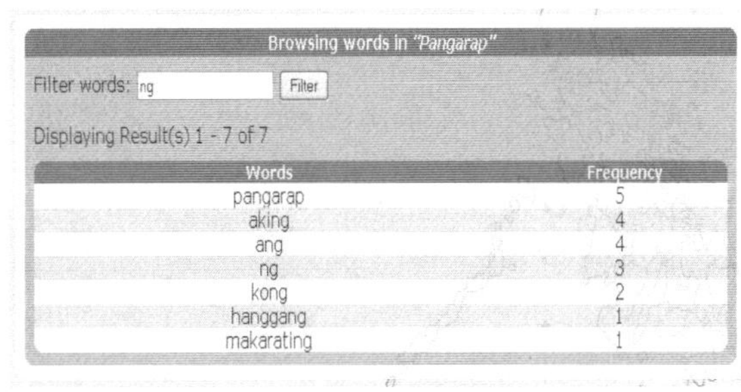

Words	Frequency
pangarap	5
aking	4
ang	4
ng	3
kong	2
hanggang	1
makarating	1

Figure 3. *Palito*'s word frequency feature

Finally, *Palito* is equipped with concordance which generates a list of the occurrences of a specific word under search. The concordance r is an indispensable tool for any corpus as it conveniently displays all occurrences of the keyword in the entire collection. Figure 4 shows how concordance works for PLOC.

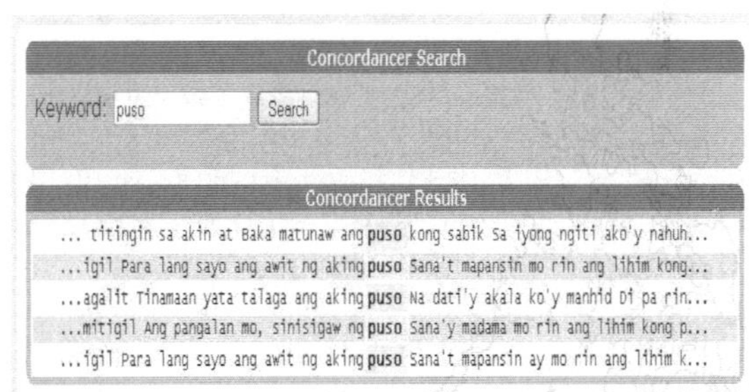

Figure 5. A screenshot of *Palito's* concordancer

Aside from the data in the Philippine corpus, the software tools will also aid language researchers everywhere in analyzing the Philippine languages, such as comparing different usages of the same word, analyzing collocates, and finding and analyzing phrases and idioms.

4 Conclusion

This paper has presented the work done so far in the building of the PLOC. As Dita et al. (2009) have reported, there were many things to consider in conceptualizing the first phase of the project. And since the primary consideration was the comparability of texts in different languages, the scope was rather limited to written genre in general, and to literary and religious texts, in particular. The second phase of the project has so far completed a 2-million word corpus of the eight major Philippine languages (Tagalog, Cebuano, Ilocano, Hiligaynon, Bicol, Kapampangan, Pangasinense, and Waray). In summary, the present PLOC now contains a 250,000-word written texts of the eight major languages in the Philippines.

There are many plans for the expansion of the PLOC. First, we plan to collect a 250,000-word counterpart in spoken texts. The spoken texts will consist of dialogues and monologues: face-to-face conversations for dialogues and speeches or radio/tv commentaries for monologues. Second, we plan to extend the coverage of written texts by including journalistic writing and other 'creative' writings such as advertisements, internet texts and the like. The plan is to get a one million-word of written and spoken corpus, for every language. If this is achieved, the expansion for the PLOC is to include as many Philippine languages as possible. When all these plans are achieved, there will be more chances of comparing features cross-linguistically, following the classic works of Blake (1906), Tsuchida, Yamada, Constantino, & Moriguchi (1989), and Constantino (1965), to name a few.

The PLOC, as it is envisioned to be, will make a significant contribution to Philippine linguistics. Doing linguistics by then, to quote Bautista (2004), would mean "sitting in one's armchair and introspecting and thinking of sample sentences to exemplify particular structures" (p. 1), as opposed to going through the laborious task of fieldwork to collect data from different informants.

Acknowledgments
This project has been partially funded by the National Commission for Culture and the Arts, Philippine Government.

References

D. Biber, S. Condrad, and R. Reppen. 1998. *Corpus linguistics: Investigating language structure and use.* Cambridge: CUP.

E. Constantino. 1965. The sentence patterns of twenty-six Philippine languages. *Lingua 15*, 71-124.

F. R. Blake. 1906. Contributions to comparative Philippine grammar (Part 1). *Journal of the American Oriental Society 27,* 317-396.

G. Leech. 1991. The state of the art in corpus linguistics. In K. Ajmer & B. Altenberg (Eds.), *English Corpus Linguistics: Linguistic Studies in Honor of Jan Svartvik,* (pp. 8-29). London: Longman.

H. Liao. 2006. Philippine linguistics: The state-of-the-art 1981-2005. Paper presented at the Annual Lecture of the Andrew Gonzalez, FSC Distinguished Professorial Chair in Linguistics and Language Education on March 4, 2006. De La Salle University, Manila, Philippines.

J. S. Quakenbush. 2005. Philippine linguistics from an SIL perspective: Trends and prospects. In H. Liao & C.R.G. Rubino (Eds.), *Current issues in Philippine linguistics and anthropology: Parangal kay Lawrence A. Reid* (pp. 3-27). Manila: Linguistic Society of the Philippines and SIL Philippines.

L. Reid. 1981. Philippine linguistics: The state of the art: 1970-1980. In D. V. Hart (Ed.), *Philippine studies: Political science, economics, and linguistics* (pp. 212-273). DeKalb: Center for Southeast Asian Studies, Northern Illinois University.

L. Reid and H. Liao. 2004. A brief syntactic typology of Philippine languages. *Language and Linguistics* 5(2), 433-490.

M. L. S. Bautista. 2004. An Overview of the Philippine Component of the International Corpus of English (ICE-PHI). *Asian Englishes*, 7(2), 8-26.

P. M. Lewis. (Ed.) 2009. *Ethnologue: Languages of the world* (16th ed.) Dallas, Tex.: SIL International. Online version: http://www.ethnologue.com/

R. Barlaan. 1986. *Some major aspects of the focus system in Isnag.* Ph.D. dissertation, University of Texas at Arlington.

Shigeru. Tsuchida, Y. Yamada, E. Constantino, and T. Moriguchi. (1989). *Batanic languages: Lists of sentences for grammatical features.* Tokyo: The University of Tokyo.

Shirley. N. Dita. 2010. A morphosyntactic analysis of the pronominal system of Philippine languages. *Proceedings of the 24th Pacific Asia Conference in Language, Information & Computation* (pp. 45-59). Tokyo: Waseda University Press.

Shirley. N. Dita, R.E.O Roxas, and P. Inventado. 2009. Building Online Corpora of Philippine Languages. *Proceedings of the Twenty-third Pacific Asia Conference on Language, Information and Computation,* 646-653.

S. Brainard. 1994. *Voice and ergativity in Karao.* Ph.D. dissertation, University of Oregon.

T. V. Ramos. 1997. *Case system of Tagalog verbs.* Ph.D. dissertation, University of Hawaii.

Providing Ad Links to Travel Blog Entries Based on Link Types

Aya ISHINO
Graduate School of Information Sciences, Hiroshima City University, Hiroshima, Japan
ishino@ls.info.hiroshima-cu.ac.jp

Hidetsugu NANBA
Graduate School of Information Sciences, Hiroshima City University, Hiroshima, Japan
nanba@hiroshima-cu.ac.jp

Toshiyuki TAKEZAWA
Graduate School of Information Sciences, Hiroshima City University, Hiroshima, Japan
takezawa@hiroshima-cu.ac.jp

Abstract

Content-targeted advertising systems are becoming an increasingly important part of the funding for free web services. These programs automatically find relevant keywords on a web page, and then display ads based on those keywords. We propose a method for providing links to ads for travel products (which we call ad links) automatically. We extract keywords from citing areas of travel information links, and provide appropriate ad links. To investigate the effectiveness of our method, we conducted experiments. We obtained a high precision for the extraction of keywords and provision of ad links.

1 Introduction

Online advertising is a form of promotion that uses the World Wide Web for the expressed purpose of delivering marketing messages to attract customers. Examples of such online ads are contextual advertising and listing advertising. Content-targeted advertising systems, such as Google's Ad Sense program and Yahoo's Contextual Match product, are becoming an increasingly important part of the funding for free web services. These programs automatically find relevant keywords on a web page, and then display ads based on those keywords. We propose a method for providing ad links for travel products to travel blog entries, which are travel journals written by bloggers in diary form. By specifying the travel domain, we aim to provide more appropriate ad links than existing content-targeted advertising systems.

To provide these ad links, we take account of the types of hyperlinks in each travel blog entry. Ishino *et al.* (2011) devised a method for constructing a collection of web links for travel information automatically. They extracted the hyperlinks by which bloggers describe useful web sites for a tourist spot from travel blog entries, and classified types of travel information link into the following four categories.

- S (Spot): The information is about tourist spots.
- H (Hotel): The information is about accommodation.
- R (Restaurant): The information is about restaurants.
- O (Other): Other than types S, H, and R.

By switching strategies for providing ad links according to these types, we attempt to provide more appropriate ad links for travel.

The remainder of this paper is organized as follows. Section 2 shows the system behavior in terms of snapshots. Section 3 discusses related work. Section 4 describes our methods. To investigate the effectiveness of our methods, we conducted some experiments, and Section 5 reports on these and the results. We present some conclusions in Section 6.

2 System Behavior

In this section, we describe our prototype system, which provides information about (1) useful web sites for tourist spots and (2) ads for travel products. The two steps in the search procedure are:

(Step 1) Input a keyword, such as "Okonomiyaki" (Japanese-style pancake), in the search form (shown as ① in Figure 1).

Proceedings of the 9th Workshop on Asian Language Resources, pages 63–70,
Chiang Mai, Thailand, November 12 and 13, 2011.

(Step 2) Click the "link" button (shown as ②) to generate a list of URLs for web sites related to the keyword together with automatically identified link types using Ishino's method (Ishino et al. 2011), the context of citations ("citing areas"), by which the authors of the travel blog entries describe the sites, and ads for travel products related to the citing areas. We classified link types into the four categories described above.

(Step 3) Click the "link"(shown as ③) to display detailed information of ads for travel products (shown in Figure 2).

We propose a method for providing ad links to travel products corresponding to the link type.

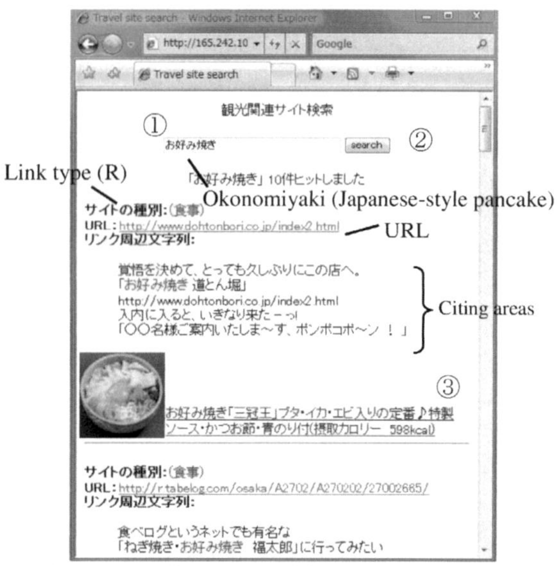

Figure 1. A list of travel information links together with automatically inserted ad links

Figure 2. An example of a web page for a travel product

3 Related Work

In this section, we describe some related studies. Recommendation systems provide a promising approach to ranking commercial products or various documents according to a user's interests. These systems can be classified into two categories by their underlying method of recommendation: (1) collaborative filtering (Goldberg *et al.* 1992) and (2) content-based filtering (Sarwar *et al.* 2000). We focus on the online advertising using the content-based filtering techniques.

Examples of online advertising are listing advertising and contextual advertising. Listing advertising is a method of placing online ads on web pages that show results from search engine queries. Search advertisements are targeted to match the entered keywords. Fujita *et al.* (2010) showed a system that automatically generates shop-specific listing ads by reusing textual data promoting each shop. They used a restaurant portal site as textual data. We use citing areas of travel information links, and provide ad links to related travel products.

In this paper, we focus on contextual advertising, which is based on keywords automatically extracted from the text of the web page. Keyword extraction is the core task of the contextual advertising system. There are a number of classical approaches to extracting keywords. TF*IDF uses a frequency criterion to select keywords. Yih *et al.* (2006) showed a learning-based technique using TF*IDF for contextual advertising. Recently, new methods based on the Wikipedia corpus have been proposed. The Wikify! system (Mihalcea and Csmomai, 2007) identifies keywords in a text, and then links these keywords to the corresponding Wikipedia pages. They identified keywords using a criterion called keyphraseness. They applied their method to English texts. We extract keywords from Japanese citing areas. Therefore, we cannot apply their method for Japanese citing areas.

4 Automatic Organization of Travel Information through Blogs

The task of organizing travel through blogs is divided into two steps: (1) classification of links in travel blog entries, and (2) providing ad links for travel information links. These steps are explained in Sections 4.1 and 4.2.

4.1 Link Classification

Ishino *et al.* (2011) devised a method for classifying links in travel blog entries into the four categories described in Section 1. The procedure is as follows.

1. Input a travel blog entry.
2. Extract a hyperlink and any surrounding sentences that mention the link (a citing area).
3. Classify the link by taking account of the information in the citing area.

In the following, we will explain Steps 2 and 3.

Extraction of citing areas
Ishino *et al.* manually created rules for the automatic extraction of citing areas. These rules use cue phrases.
Method of link type classification
They classified hyperlinks automatically. They employed a machine-learning technique using the following features. Here, a sequence of nouns (a noun phrase) was treated as a noun.

- A word.
- Whether the word is a cue phrase, detailed as follows, where the numbers in brackets shown for each feature represent the number of cues (shown in Table 1, Table 2, and Table 3).

Cue phrase	Number of cues
A list of tourist spots, collected from Wikipedia	17,371
Words frequently used in the names of tourist spots, such as "動物園" (zoo) or "博物館" (museum)	138
Words related to sightseeing, such as "見学" (sightseeing) or "散策" (stroll)	172
Other words	131

Table 1. Cues for type S

Cue phrase	Number of cues
Words frequently used in the name of hotels, such as "ホテル" (hotel) or "旅館" (Japanese inn)	9
Component words for accommodation, such as "フロント" (front desk) or "客室" (guest room)	29
Words frequently used when tourists stay in accommodation, such as "泊る" (stay) or "チェックイン" (check in)	14
Other words.	21

Table 2. Cues for type H

Cue phrase	Number of cues
Dish names such as "omelet", collected from Wikipedia	2,779
Cooking styles such as "Italian cuisine", collected from Wikipedia	114
Words frequently used in the names of restaurants, such as "レストラン" (restaurant) or "食堂" (dining room)	21
Words used when taking meals, such as "食べる" (eat) or "おいしい" (delicious).	52
General words that indicate food, such as "ご飯" (rice) or "料理" (cooking)	31
Other words	31

Table 3. Cues for type R

To investigate the effectiveness of their method, Ishino *et al.* conducted an experiment. The evaluation results are shown in Table 4. We applied this model to 17,266 travel blog entries, and classified 4,155 links. The numbers of automatically classified links are shown in Table 5. We call these links travel information links. We describe the method for providing ad links to travel products in the following section.

Link types	Recall (%)	Precision (%)
S	62.5	72.7
H	64.9	81.3
R	71.9	76.7
O	71.6	48.6

Table 4. Evaluation results for link classification (Ishino *et al.* 2011)

Link types	S	H	R	O
Number of links	1,174	123	921	2,061

Table 5. The number of links of each type

4.2 Providing Ad Links for Travel Information Links

The procedure for providing ad links for travel information links is as follows.

1. Input a link type and the citing areas of a travel information link.
2. Extract keywords from the citing areas.
3. Extract product data containing all keywords, and calculate the similarity be-

tween the citing areas of a travel information link and the product data.

4. Provide an ad link to the product data having the highest similarity for the travel information link.

In the following, we will explain Steps 2 and 3.

Keyword extraction based on link types

We extract keywords for travel products corresponding to the link type. We use the cues used by Ishino's method for classifying travel information links, and extract keywords from citing areas of link types S and R.

First, we describe the method for extracting keywords from citing areas of link type S. The cues for type S shown in Table 1, such as tourist spots collected from Wikipedia and words frequently used in the names of tourist spots, tend to become keywords. Therefore, we register these cues as candidate keywords for link type S. If citing areas of link type S contain candidate keywords, we extract them as keywords. In addition, if citing areas contain names of places, we extract them as keywords. Candidate keywords for link type S are shown in Table 6.

Next, we describe a method for extracting keywords from citing areas of link type R. The cue for type R shown in Table 3, such as dish names and cooking styles, tend to become keywords. Therefore, we register these cues as candidate keywords for link type R. If citing areas of link type R contain candidate keywords, we extract them as keywords. Candidate keywords for link type R are shown in Table 7. We used CabOCha software (http://chasen.org/~taku/software/cabocha/) to identify location names.

Candidate keywords	Number of candidate keywords
A list of tourist spots, collected from Wikipedia	17,812
Words frequently used in the names of tourist spots, such as "動物園" (zoo) or "博物館" (museum)	138
Names of places	

Table 6. Candidate keywords for link type S

Candidate keywords	Number of candidate keywords
Dish names such as "omelet", collected from Wikipedia	2,779
Cooking styles such as "Italian cuisine", collected from Wikipedia	114

Table 7. Candidate keywords for link type R

Product data extraction based on the link types

We extract product data, which contain all keywords, and calculate the similarity between citing areas of a travel information link and the product data.

Product data

We provide ad links to travel products of Rakuten Shopping Mall (Rakuten Ichiba) or facility data of Rakuten Travel released through the Rakuten Institute of Technology for travel information links. An example of product data of Rakuten Ichiba is shown in Figure 3. The product data contain 50 million items. An item has a name, a code, a price, descriptive texts, URL, picture, shop code, category ID and registration date. The facility data contain 11,468 facilities. A facility data entry has a name, ID number, and user review.

	Product data
Name	[marine diving] Earthly paradise OKINAWA 2009
Code	seasir-umi:10001011
Price	980
Descriptive text	*The guidebook contains extended information about diving in Okinawa! *It introduces 140 dive spots!
URL	http://item.rakuten.co.jp/seasir-umi/r023/
Picture	@0_mall/seasir-umi/cabinet/09shohin/rakuenokinawa_2009.jpg
Category ID	101922
Registration date	2010/03/24 15:08:58

Figure 3. Product data

We provide ad links to product data having associations with travel information links by using the link types of the travel information links. We take account of the characteristics of link types, and assign each category to link types. Categories of product data are shown in Table 8.

Facility data do not contain descriptive texts about the facilities. Therefore, we proposed a method for providing ad links for travel information links of link types S and R.

Link types	Category	Number of product data items
S (Spot)	Product data related to travel.	51,516
H (Hotel)	Facility data.	11,468
R (Restaurant)	Product data related to food.	830,807

Table 8. Category of product data assigned to each link type.

We describe a method for collecting product data related to travel. Product data has a category ID. A category master, shown in Table 9, was released through the Rakuten Institute of Technology. The category master has a hierarchic structure. First, we collect subcategories of the category "Travel, Study abroad, Outdoor amusement". In this way, we collect category IDs related to travel, and show the category IDs in Table 10. Next, we collect product data with category ID related to travel as product data related to travel. In the same way, we collect product data related to food.

Category ID	Category name	Subcategory ID
101242	Travel, Study abroad, Outdoor amusement	200162
209835	SANYO	209830
503221	Panasonic	503218

Table 9. The category master

Category ID	Category name
208922	Hot spring
208924	Theme park
208925	Guidebook
208930	Travel book, Travel essay
411387	Mountain climbing, Outdoor amusement, Camp

Table 10. Category IDs related to travel

Similarity calculation

We describe the method for calculating the similarity between citing areas and product data. We extract product data that contain all keywords *K*, and calculate the similarity *Score* between citing areas of a travel information link and the product data. *Score* is calculated as follows:

$$Score = \sum_{k_i \subseteq K} Link\_Score(k_i) * Advertising\_Score(k_i) \qquad (1)$$

Link_Score(k_i) is the number of times the given keywords k_i appears in that citing area. *Advertising_Score(k_i)* is the number of times the given keyword k_i appears in the descriptive text of the product data. We provide an ad link to the product having the highest score for the travel information link.

5 Experiments

To investigate the effectiveness of our methods, we conducted several experiments.

5.1 Experimental Method

To generate the test data for providing ad links, we randomly selected 50 travel information links of type S and 50 of type R and manually classified them. To investigate the effectiveness of our method, we extracted keywords using the following two methods for evaluation of keywords in Section 5.2 and ad links in Section 5.3.

- Our method: Extract keywords by our method, as described in Section 4.2.
- TF*IDF: TF*IDF is a conventional baseline used in the scientific literature for comparison of keywords extraction algorithms. IDF was calculated using an open API (http://developer.yahoo.co.jp/webapi/search/websearch/v2/websearch.html). We extract the top-X words as keywords.

In addition, we evaluated our method for ad links for the limited categories described in Section 4.2 and all categories of product data.

5.2 Evaluation of Keywords

We evaluated the method for keywords extraction. We used precision as the evaluation measure, calculated as follows:

$$\text{Precision} = \frac{\text{the number of appropriaive keywords}}{\text{the number of extravted keywords}} \qquad (2)$$

The evaluation results are shown in Table 11. Our method attained higher precision than baseline methods.

	Link Type S (%)	Link Type R (%)
Our method	**81.8 (72/88)**	**98.0 (49/50)**
TF*IDF(X=1)	46.0 (23/50)	48.0 (24/50)
TF*IDF(X=2)	38.0 (38/100)	37.4 (37/99)
TF*IDF(X=3)	36.0 (54/150)	36.5 (54/148)
TF*IDF(X=4)	34.0 (68/200)	31.5 (62/197)
TF*IDF(X=5)	34.0 (85/250)	32.5 (80/246)

Table 11.Precision of extracted keywords

There were two typical errors in keyword extraction: (1) the lack of cues and (2) a problem with the method of keywords extraction. We describe these errors as follows.

(1) The lack of cues:
For keywords extraction, we used manually selected cues, as described in Section 4.2. To improve the coverage of cues, a statistical approach, such as applying n-gram statistics to a larger blog corpus, will be required.

(2) The problem with the method of keywords extraction:
In the following example, our method mistakenly extracted "天然温泉" (a natural hot spring) as a keyword, because the candidate keywords for link type S "天然温泉" (a natural hot spring) appears in the citing areas.

[original]
お湯のヌルヌル感と温まり具合は最高です。
高浜の「湯っぷる」
詳しいことは→
http://www.seaside-takahama.com/
ここは天然温泉じゃないんですが
[translation]
The quality and the temperature of spring water are great.
"YUPPLE" in Takahama.
For details, access the following web page:
http://www.seaside-takahama.com/
YUPPLE is not a natural hot spring.

5.3 Evaluation of Ad Links

We evaluated the method for providing ad links for travel information links. We used precision and coverage as evaluation measures, which were calculated as follows:

$$\text{Precision} = \frac{\text{the number of appropriative travel information links provided ad links}}{\text{the number of travel information links provided ad links}} \quad (3)$$

$$\text{Coverage} = \frac{\text{the number of travel information links provided ad links}}{\text{the number of travel information links}} \quad (4)$$

The evaluation results are shown in Table 12 and Table 13. We obtained a higher precision than the baseline methods.

	Precision (%)	Coverage (%)
Our method	**79.3 (23/29)**	**58.0 (29/50)**
TF*IDF(X=1)	39.1 (18/46)	92.0 (46/50)
TF*IDF(X=2)	37.8 (14/37)	74.0 (37/50)
TF*IDF(X=3)	35.9 (7/20)	40.0 (20/50)
TF*IDF(X=4)	36.4 (4/11)	22.0 (11/50)
TF*IDF(X=5)	0.0 (0/2)	4.0 (2/50)

Table 12. Precision and coverage of providing ad links for travel information links of type S

	Precision (%)	Coverage (%)
Our method	**91.3 (21/23)**	**46.0 (23/50)**
TF*IDF(X=1)	22.0 (11/50)	100.0 (50/50)
TF*IDF(X=2)	29.5 (13/44)	88.0 (44/50)
TF*IDF(X=3)	25.0 (7/28)	56.0 (28/50)
TF*IDF(X=4)	6.3 (1/16)	32.0 (16/50)
TF*IDF(X=5)	25.0 (2/8)	16.5 (8/50)

Table 13. Precision and coverage of providing ad links for travel information links of type R

First, we discuss the results for link type S. As shown in Table 12, our method attained higher precision than the baseline methods. For coverage, TF*IDF (X=1) and TF*IDF (X=2) were better than our method, while we obtained more appropriate travel information links provided as ad links than the baseline method.

Next, we discuss the results for link type R. As shown in Table 13, our method attained higher precision than the baseline methods. For coverage, TF*IDF (X=1), TF*IDF (X=2) and TF*IDF (X=3) were better than our method, while we obtained larger numbers of appropriate travel information links provided as ad links than the baseline methods. Therefore, our experimental results confirm the effectiveness of our methods.

We discuss a typical error in providing links. In the following example, we could not provide ad links. Our method extracted an appropriative keyword "Nihon-heso-kōen" (The Navel Park,

NISHIWAKI, JAPAN). Nihon-heso-kōen is a park in Hyogo prefecture, Japan. However, there are no product data containing this word, and we could not provide any ad links for the travel information link. To solve this problem, we took the address of Nihon-heso-kōen from web pages, and provided an ad link to a guidebook that describes tourist spots near Nihon-heso-kōen for the travel information link.

[original]
今回初めてお会いした、Kamon さん奥さんは、モデルさんのようなとても綺麗な方でした！
このメンバーで、第一目的地”日本へそ公園”へ
ここでの目的は、やっぱり”ぶーにゃん”に会う事・・・
が、今回も会えませんでしたつ
Д｀)・゜・。・゜゜・*:.。

[translation]
I met with Mrs. Kamon for the first time. She was very beautiful like a model!
We came to visit "Nihon-heso-kōen" (The Navel Park, NISHIWAKI, JAPAN).
We expected to see "Bu-nyan", but we missed again :-(

5.4 Evaluation of Limited Category

We evaluate our method for ad links for the limited category shown in Section 4.2 and for all categories of product data. We used precision and coverage as evaluation measures, as described in Section 4.3. The evaluation results are shown in Table 14 and Table 15.

	Precision (%)	Coverage (%)
Our method (particular category)	79.3 (23/29)	58.0 (29/50)
Baseline (all categories)	38.2 (13/34)	68.0 (34/50)

Table 14. Precision and coverage of ad links for travel information links of type S (evaluation particular category)

	Precision (%)	Coverage (%)
Our method (particular category)	91.3 (21/23)	46.0 (23/50)
Baseline (all categories)	70.8 (17/24)	48.0 (24/50)

Table 15. Precision and coverage of ad links for travel information links of type R (evaluation of particular category)

As shown in the tables, our method attained higher precision than the baseline method. For coverage, baselines of types S and R were better than our method, while we obtained a larger number of appropriate travel information links provided as ad links than the baseline method. Therefore, our experimental results confirm the effectiveness of our methods.

As examples of more appropriate ad links than our method could provide, the baseline method could provide ad links to product data not directly related to travel, such as books, CDs and DVDs that describe tourist spots. These are not categorized as product data related to travel in our system. In our future work, we plan to classify such product data as related to travel automatically so that we can provide more appropriate ad links.

6 Conclusion

We have proposed a method for providing ad links for travel information links automatically. For the extraction of keywords, we obtained 81.8% precision for link type S and 98.0% precision for link type R. For providing ad links, we obtained 79.3% precision for link type S and 78.3% precision for link type R. Our method also provided larger numbers of appropriate travel information links as ad links than the baseline method. Our experimental results have confirmed the effectiveness of our methods.

7 Future Work

For our method, we used manually selected cues. To increase the number of cues, a statistical approach is required.

In this paper, we have focused on travel information links written in Japanese. In our future work, we will translate cue phrases from Japanese into other languages, and apply our method to travel information links in various languages.

Reference

Aya Ishino, Hidetsugu Nanba, and Toshiyuki Takezawa. 2011. Automatic Compilation of an Online Travel Portal from Automatically Extracted Travel Blog Entries. *Proceedings of ENTER 2011*, 113-124.

Hidetsugu Nanba, Haruka Taguma, Takahiro Ozaki, Daisuke Kobayashi, Aya Ishino, and Toshiyuki Takezawa. 2009. Automatic Compilation of Travel Information from Automatically Identified Travel Blogs. *Proceedings of the Joint Conference of the 47th Annual Meeting of the Association for Computational Linguistics and the 4th International Joint Conference on Natural Language Processing, Short Paper*, 205-208.

Atsushi Fujita, Katsuhiro Ikushima, Satoshi Sato, Ryo Kamite, Ko Ishiyama, and Osamu Tamachi. 2010. Automatic Generation of Listing Ads by Reusing Promotional Texts. *Proceedings of the 12th International Conference on Electronic Commerce (ICEC)*, 191-200.

David Goldberg, David Nichols, Brian M. Oki, and Douglas Terry. 1992. Using Collaborative Filtering to Weave an Information Tapestry. *Communications of the ACM*, 35(12), 61-70.

Badrul Sarwar, George Karypis, Joseph Konstan, and John Riedl. 2000. Analysis of Recommendation Algorithms for E-commerce. *Proceedings of the 2nd ACM Conference on Electronic Commerce*, 158-167.

Wen-tau Yih, Joshua Goodman, and Vitor R. Carvalho. 2006. Finding Advertising Keywords on Web Pages. *Proceedings of the 15th International Conference on World Wide Web.*

Rada Mihalcea and Andras Csomai. 2007. Wikify!: Linking Documents to Encyclopedic Knowledge. *Proceedings of the 16th ACM Conference on Information and Knowledge Management*, 233-242.

Towards a Computational Semantic Analyzer for Urdu

Annette Hautli **Miriam Butt**
Department of Linguistics
University of Konstanz
{annette.hautli|miriam.butt}@uni-konstanz.de

Abstract

This paper describes a first approach to a computational semantic analyzer for Urdu on the basis of the deep syntactic analysis done by the Urdu grammar ParGram. Apart from the semantic construction, external lexical resources such as an Urdu WordNet and a preliminary VerbNet style resource for Urdu are developed and connected to the semantic analyzer. These resources allow for a deeper level of representation by providing real-word knowledge such as hypernyms of lexical entities and information on thematic roles. We therefore contribute to the overall goal of providing more insights into the computationally efficient analysis of Urdu, in particular to computational semantic analysis.

1 Introduction

The state of the art in wide-coverage deep syntactic parsing has allowed semantic processing to come within reach of applications in computational linguistics (Bos et al., 2004). This new possibility for wide-coverage computational semantic analysis however also raises questions about appropriate meaning representations as well as engineering issues. We address some of these here.

In achieving the goal of producing a deep, broad-coverage semantic analysis for text, much effort has been put into the development of robust and broad-coverage syntactic and semantic parsers as well as lexical resources. However, the focus has mostly been on European languages.

For Urdu, neither a wide-coverage computational semantic analyzer nor a wealth of lexical resources exist to date; however, efforts have been put into the development of a syntactic parser within the framework of Lexical-Functional Grammar (LFG) (Bresnan and Kaplan, 1982; Dalrymple, 2001), namely the Urdu ParGram Grammar (Butt and King, 2002; Bögel et al., 2007; Bögel et al., 2009). As to the development of lexical resources, Ahmed and Hautli (2010) have generated a preliminary Urdu WordNet on the basis of Hindi WordNet (Bhattacharyya, 2010). A lexical resource for Urdu verbs following the methodology of the English VerbNet (Kipper-Schuler, 2005) is currently under construction, some of its content has already been hooked into the our Urdu semantic analyzer Urdu (section 2.2.2).

The computationally efficient semantic analysis of Urdu is a completely new area of research and it is not immediately clear what a cross-linguistically motivated representation and analysis should look like. Therefore, the aim of this paper is to present a first approach to a computational semantic representation of Urdu and to discuss some of the challenges that have to be dealt with. In addition we show how external lexical resources can be linked to the system and discuss what information these lexical resources contribute to the overall semantic analysis.

The paper is structured as follows: Section 2 elaborates on some of the resources available for Urdu, followed by a detailed description of the semantic analyzer in Section 3. Section 4 elaborates on some of the issues involved in building the system, followed by the conclusion in Section 5.

2 Concepts

2.1 The Urdu ParGram Grammar

The Urdu LFG grammar (Butt and King, 2002; Bögel et al., 2007; Bögel et al., 2009) is part of an international research program called ParGram (Parallel Grammars) (Butt et al., 2002), aiming at developing parallel syntactic analyses for different languages within the LFG framework (Butt et al., 1999). The underlying platform that is used to

Proceedings of the 9th Workshop on Asian Language Resources, pages 71–78,
Chiang Mai, Thailand, November 12 and 13, 2011.

develop parallel LFG grammars is XLE (Crouch et al., 2011), developed at Palo Alto Research Center (PARC) and consisting of cutting-edge algorithms for parsing and generating LFG grammars along with a user interface for writing and debugging.

LFG postulates two basic levels of syntactic description for natural language utterances. Phrase structure configurations (linear order, constituency and hierarchical relations) are represented in a *constituent structure* (c-structure), whereas grammatical functions are explicitly represented at the other level of description, the *functional structure* (f-structure), an attribute value matrix (AVM).

Building XLE grammars involves the manual writing of syntactic rules that are annotated with f-structure information. It is possible to incorporate a stochastic disambiguation module into the grammar (Riezler et al., 2002), but this still needs to be done for the Urdu grammar. The amount of manual work makes grammar development a higher-level task, whose positive side is the integration of theoretically well informed analyses that hold generally across languages.

However, grammar rules are not the only component of an XLE grammar. Figure 1 provides an overview of the complete processing pipeline.

tokenizer & morphology (FST)
↓
transliteration (FST)
↓
syntax (XLE LFG)
↓
semantics (XFR ORDERED REWRITING)

Figure 1: Urdu XLE pipeline

At first, sentences are tokenized into words, these words are transliterated into a Roman version of the Arabic script (Malik et al., 2010) and then morphologically analyzed by a finite-state morphological analyzer (Bögel et al., 2007). The transliteration allows us to abstract away from some of the vagaries of the Urdu script as well as open up our grammar for the processing and generation of Hindi (cf. section 2.2.1).

The information gained from the morphological analyzer is passed on to the XLE syntax component, where the grammar rules generate c- and f-structure. The semantic XFR system will be presented in full detail in Section 3. Note that it is possible to reverse the pipeline and generate back out from an f-structure analysis (but not as yet from a semantic representation).

This syntactically deep approach is particularly well suited for languages with fairly free word order, such as Urdu, as it looks beyond the surface arrangement of words in a sentence and provides a deep functional and semantic analysis. As an example, see Figure 2 for a c- and f-structure of (1).

(1) اس نے تل آبیب میں سیب کھایا
us nE t3ul AbEb mEN sEb kHAyA
he Erg Tel Aviv in apple eat.Perf.F.Sg
'He ate an apple in Tel Aviv.'

The level we are most concerned with is the f-structure, as it is a first step towards a semantic analysis (f-structures have been shown to be equivalent to quasi logical forms; (van Genabith and Crouch, 1996)). In cases where parts of constituents are scattered across the sentence, e.g., as in discontinuous parts of an NP (Raza and Ahmed, 2011), the f-structure collects these pieces in the one grammatical function representation they belong to. This greatly facilitates the automatic semantic analysis because we can build on a deep and very detailed syntactic analysis that already abstracts from the surface sentential order.

Looking at Figure 2, the c-structure is shown on the left and models the linear order and hierarchical relationshiop of the constituents. In the AVM on the right, the f-structure, the main predicate of the sentence is *kHA* 'to eat', the subject (SUBJ) of the sentence is the pronoun *us* 'he/she', with the object (OBJ) *sEb* 'apple'. The location is analysed as an adjunct, an optional element in the sentence. Information on tense and aspect is captured in the TNS-ASP f-structure at the bottom. There is also some lexical semantic information contained in the analysis under LEX-SEM, namely that it is an agentive, ingestive verb.[1]

In addition to the f-structure, a computational semantic analysis abstracts even further away from the syntax and is able to provide information on the lexical semantics of the words involved by supplementing the analysis with information from external lexical resources, see section 3.

2.2 Lexical Resources for Urdu

2.2.1 Urdu WordNet

Due to the resource sparseness in Indo-Aryan languages, there are only a few lexical resources

[1]The CHECK feature collects grammar internal features for well-formedness checking and can be filtered out.

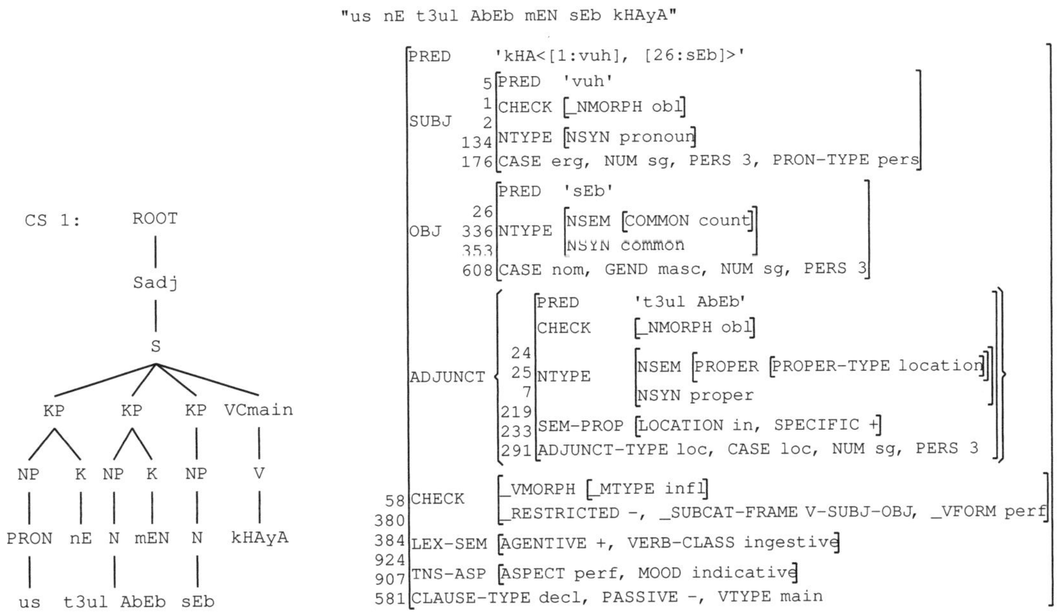

Figure 2: C- and f-structure for *us nE t3ul AbEb mEN sEb kHAyA* 'He ate an apple in Tel Aviv.'

already available, one of them Hindi Wordnet (Bhattacharyya et al., 2008; Bhattacharyya, 2010) which is inspired in methodology and architecture by the English WordNet (Fellbaum, 1998). Fortunately, Urdu and Hindi are structurally almost identical, although the two writing systems (a version of Arabic and Devanagari, respectively) differ markedly. This difference can be overcome by employing a transliterator from Arabic to Roman script and vice versa (Malik et al., 2010), combining it with a transliterator that maps Roman to Devanagari script (also vice versa), using XFST by (Beesley and Karttunen, 2003). Figure 3 sketches the pipeline of how we arrive at a preliminary Urdu WordNet (Ahmed and Hautli, 2010).

Urdu input
↓
transliteration to Hindi
↓
lookup in Hindi WordNet
↓
extraction of Hindi WordNet information
↓
removing synset description and example
↓
basic lexical resource for Urdu

Figure 3: Hindi/Urdu WordNet pipeline

By using this methodology it is possible to generate a preliminary Urdu WordNet (Ahmed and Hautli, 2010) that can be employed in various NLP applications, among them the semantic representation presented in this paper. A sample output for the noun *sEb* 'apple' is shown in Figure 4.

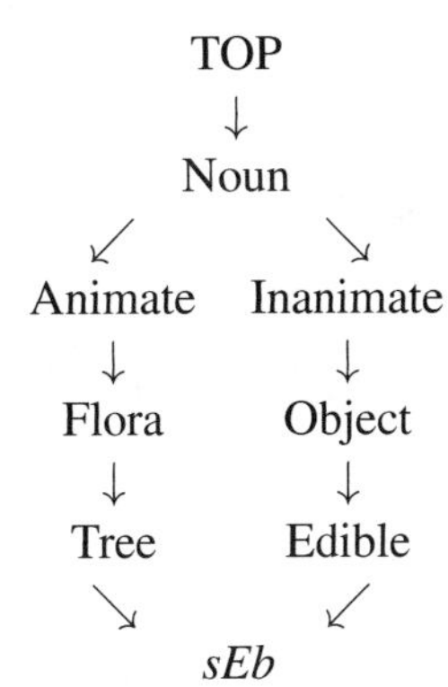

Figure 4: Sample Urdu WordNet output

First experiments have shown that this approach is a promising first step towards creating a basic lexical ontology for Urdu, however a thoroughly worked out Urdu WordNet will require additional work. For one, lexical items that are Hindi-specific will need to be flagged and words that are Urdu-specific will need to be introduced. In particular, the ezafe construction (Butt et al., 2008), illustrated in (2), will need to be dealt with. However, this is not trivial, as the ezafe *e* is often not written in Urdu, as is indeed the case in (2).

(2) وزیر اعظم
vazir-e azAm
minister.M.Sg-Ezafe great
'the prime minister' (lit. the great minister)

2.2.2 Towards a resource for Urdu verbs

One lexical resource used by the English LFG grammar is the English VerbNet (Kipper-Schuler, 2005), which categorizes English verbs according to Levin's verb classes (Levin, 1993). On the one hand, verbs are grouped according to their semantic relatedness, e.g. ingestive verbs or verbs of motion. Moreover, these related verbs are grouped into further subclasses according to their syntactic behavior. In addition to this semantic and syntactic classification, VerbNet also encodes information on the event structure and the thematic roles (Fillmore, 1985) of a verb. A similar resource is being developed for Hindi (Begum et al., 2008), however instead of Western style thematic roles, Panini's *karaka* relations are used.

For Urdu, we are currently working on creating a VerbNet style resource, carefully taking into account the characteristics of Urdu verbs regarding their syntactic behavior and including sufficient lexical semantic information so that the resource can be used in NLP tools. At the moment, most of the classification work is done by hand, because we also want to capture the very subtle variations which are likely to be lost in an automatic approach. For the case at hand, we are particularly interested in getting information on the thematic roles of a verb.

As an example, we consider the *rakH* 'put' class. A subgroup of these verbs allow for a locative alternation illustrated in (3)–(4). For the automatic semantic analysis it is solely important that the correct thematic roles are assigned to the arguments of the verb. Therefore we have to include this information in the verb resource for Urdu. By combining the information coming from the f-structure, where, for example, a locative adjunct is marked as such, with the information coming from the lexical resource, we can arrive at a semantic analysis that represents concepts rather than the actual sentence.

(3) میں نے گلاس میں پانی بھرا
mEN=nE gilAs mEN pAnI bHarA
I=Erg glas.M.Sg in water.M.Sg fill.Perf.M.Sg
'I filled water in the glass.'

⟨Agent, Theme, Location⟩

(4) میں نے پانی سے گلاس بھرا
mEN=nE pAnI=sE gilAs bHarA
I=Erg water.M.Sg=Instr glass.Nom fill.Perf.M.Sg
I filled the glass with water.

⟨Agent, Location, Theme⟩

The group of verbs in this class are: ڈھانپ DHANp 'to cover', بھر bHar 'to fill', سج saj 'to get decorated' and ڈھک DHak 'to cover'.

3 Urdu computational semantic analysis

3.1 General methodology

The primary aim of the semantic analyzer is to provide a more abstract level of linguistic representation, building on the information that is coming from the syntax, particularly from the f-structure. The Prolog-based XFR rewrite rules offer a suitable method for XLE grammars to arrive at a semantic representation (Crouch and King, 2006). Although they operate mainly on f-structures, c-structure information can also be used, e.g. to investigate scope issues further.

The XFR system is a language-independent component of XLE that can be used for various tasks, e.g. machine translation or the mapping of f-structures to semantic representations. The XFR semantic representation is driven neither by a specific semantic theory about meaning representation, nor by a theoretically motivated apparatus of meaning construction. It is a computational solution, which is why it is seen as a "semantic conversion" rathern than a "semantic construction".

XFR comprises a set of rewrite rules, the facts on the left hand side of a rule are rewritten to the facts on the right hand side. In addition, the rewrite rules are ordered, i.e. the first rule applies to the original input, the second rule takes as input the output of the first rule and so on.

For a concrete example of an XFR rewrite rule, we consider the f-structure in Figure 2. Given the case that we would want to systematically replace the subject and the object of the sentence with the right corresponding thematic roles, we could employ the rule in Figure 5.

```
PRED(%1,kHA), SUBJ(%1,%2), OBJ(%1,%3)
==>
context_head(%1,kHA),
role(Agent,kHA,%2),
role(Patient,kHA,%3).
```

Figure 5: Example of an XFR rewrite rule

The matrix f-structure is represented by the variable `%1`, its `SUBJ` f-structure is stored under variable `%2`, the `OBJ` under variable `%3`. If the facts do not match correctly, the rule does not apply. If the rule applies, the facts on the left hand side are consumed and rewritten to the facts on the right hand side of the rule. The representation that is generated is a flat representation of the predicate argument structure of the clause, i.e. it is not distributed across f-structures, . Despite the oversimplifying nature of the rule in Figure 5, the methodology remains the same for more complex rule constructions. In the following we present a more complex XFR rule.

3.2 The Urdu XFR system

Figure 6 presents a schematic view of the Urdu semantics pipeline.

syntax (XLE LFG)
↓
semantics (XFR ORDERED REWRITING)
↑
inclusion of lexical resources
(XFR ORDERED REWRITING)

Figure 6: Urdu Semantics pipeline

Input to the semantic representation is the syntactic XLE analysis as shown in Figure 2, which is stored in a Prolog format and can then be further processed by the XFR system. The output of the XFR semantic rules is shown in Figure 7. This representation does not yet contain information coming from lexical resources yet; its inclusion will be discussed in greater detail in Section 3.3.

In the semantic representation at hand, the sentential predicate *kHA* 'eat' is the `context_head` of the semantic representation, a term which is equivalent to the notion of the main predication in the formal semantics literature. The subcategorized arguments in the sentence are rewritten to `role` facts, the default roles of `sem_subj` and `sem_obj` will later be replaced by the thematic roles coming from the verb lexical resource.

Another main factor of the semantic analysis in that one should be able to see the domain of predication, i.e. the contexts in which the predications of the sentence hold. In the case at hand, there is only one context where predications can be true, namely context `t` (`in_context(t, ...)`) with its head *kHA* 'eat' (`context_head(t,kHA:87)`).[2]

Main clauses as well as relative clauses and other subordinate clauses open up new contexts in which predications are true or false. These clauses can be identified due to the syntactic analysis at f-structure level, where they are analyzed as COMPs or XCOMPs (complementizers). Lexical items such as negation markers also open up new contexts, e.g. the negation *nahIN* 'not'. By checking which predications hold in which contexts, sophisticated analyses of facts vs. beliefs and modal contexts can be achieved.

Another very important component of the syntactic as well as the semantic analysis is the inclusion of named entities in the lexicon. Hautli and Sulger (2011) have used automatic methods on a raw Urdu corpus to detect these so-called multiwords and also to classify them. They are very important for the system, because the components have a non-compositional meaning and should be treated as one unit.

This becomes apparent when looking at the predicate of the `ADJUNCT`, *t3ul AbEb* 'Tel Aviv'. It is analyzed as one unit and is the bare modifier of the verb phrase (`bare_mod(kHA:87, 't3ul AbEb':41)`). Due to the f-structure information [`PROPER-TYPE location`], it is clear that the modifier is locative, which is captured by the fact (`proper_name't3ul AbEb', location`).

The `skolem_info` facts store the part-of-speech information for each lexical item in the sentence and are the prerequisite for looking up words in lexical resources. The `original_fsattr` facts provide information according to which ambiguous information from the lexical resources can be disambiguated. The information about the subcategorization frame (`subcat`) is kept for the same reason, in case where a verb has multiple frames in the lexical resource, the system can choose the appropriate one according the subcategorization information coming from the syntax.

In cases where multiple valid semantic representations are generated, all analyses are displayed. Disambiguation on that level would require a more discourse-oriented analysis, which we do not provide at the moment.

[2]The numeral after each lexical item is simply a feature of bookkeeping, so that lexical items occurring twice in a sentence can be distinguished.

```
cf(1, context_head(t,kHA:87)),
cf(1, in_context(t,perf(kHA:87))),
cf(1, in_context(t,cardinality(sEb:70,sg))),
cf(1, in_context(t,cardinality('t3ul AbEb':41,sg))),
cf(1, in_context(t,cardinality(vuh:0,sg))),
cf(1, in_context(t,proper_name('t3ul AbEb':41,location,'t3ul AbEb')),
cf(1, in_context(t,role('sem_subj',kHA:87,vuh:0))),
cf(1, in_context(t,role('sem_obj',kHA:87,sEb:70))),
cf(1, in_context(t,role(bare_mod,kHA:87,'t3ul AbEb':41))),
cf(1, name_source('t3ul AbEb':41,lex)),
cf(1, name_type('t3ul AbEb':41,location)),
cf(1, original_fsattr('ADJUNCT',kHA:87,'t3ul AbEb':41)),
cf(1, original_fsattr('OBJ',kHA:87,sEb:70)),
cf(1, original_fsattr('SUBJ',kHA:87,vuh:0)),
cf(1, original_fsattr(gender,'t3ul AbEb':41,'-')),
cf(1, original_fsattr(human,'t3ul AbEb':41,'-')),
cf(1, original_fsattr(subcat,kHA:87,'V-SUBJ-OBJ')),
cf(1, skolem_info(kHA:87,kHA,verb,verb,t)),
cf(1, skolem_info(sEb:70,sEb,noun,common,t)),
cf(1, skolem_info('t3ul AbEb':41,'t3ul AbEb',name,location,t)),
cf(1, skolem_info(vuh:0,vuh,noun,pronoun,t)),
cf(1, subcat(kHA:87,'V-SUBJ-OBJ'))
```

Figure 7: Semantic representation for *us nE t3ul AbEb meN sEb kHAyA* 'He ate an apple in Tel Aviv.'

3.3 The inclusion of lexical resources

This section deals more closely with the inclusion of external lexical semantic information, making the general XFR methodology quite a powerful one because knowledge from various sources can be combined in one system.

By including knowledge contained in an Urdu WordNet and the Urdu verb resource, we can include hypernym relations such as that an apple is a fruit or the thematic roles of the arguments in a clause. This abstraction is not on the syntactic level any more, but is now at the level of lexical semantics. The benefit of such a representation is that we arrive at a meta-level of analysis where concepts are represented rather than linguistic structure.

For Urdu WordNet, we consider all senses that are produced for one item by the resource (i.e. see the two different senses for *sEb* 'apple' in Figure 4) and we take the direct hypernym of the lexical item. For the verb resource, we are mainly concerned with the thematic roles that are assigned to the arguments of the sentence.

In order to include external resources, they are reformatted as non-resourced Prolog facts (template name `uwn` for information from Urdu WordNet and `verbs` for thematic role information in Figure 8) that can be picked up by the XFR rewrite rules. For that, the templates are called on the right side of an XFR rule and compared with the information from the semantic representation. If the information matches, the rule applies and the lexical items are rewritten to include the conceptual information from the lexical resources.

See Figure 8 for an example of non-resourced facts that are being called by XFR rules and that rewrite information coming from the semantic representation in Figure 7. If the context head of the sentence is *kHA* 'eat' in a context with a variable `%Ctx`[3], and if within the same context `%Ctx` there is a semantic subject with variable `%S` and a semantic object with variable `%O` that are also captured in the `original_fsattr` and the `skolem_info` facts and given that the verb is found in the non-resourced facts, then rewrite the arguments to their thematic roles.

The second rewrite rule includes information from Urdu WordNet and inserts the hypernym of the verb *kHA* 'eat', namely that it is a verb of consumption.

The resulting semantic representation is presented in a less formal way in Figure 9. The Agent of the sentence, *vuh* 'he/she' performs a consumptive action, *kHA* 'eat' towards the Patient, *sEb* 'apple' and this act is performed at the location *t3ul AbEb* 'Tel Aviv'.

[3]The '+' in front of the first fact keeps the fact from being rewritten and can be called in later rule sequences.

```
|-uwn(kHA,Consumption);
|-verbs(kHA,Agent,Patient);

+context_head(%Ctx,kHA),
in_context(%Ctx,role(sem_subj,kHA,%S),
in_context(%Ctx,role(sem_obj,kHA,%O),
original_fsattr(SUBJ,%Pred,%S),
original_fsattr(OBJ,%Pred,%O),
skolem_info(kHA,kHA,verb,verb,%Ctx),
skolem_info(%O,%O,noun,common,%Ctx)),
skolem_info(%S,%S,noun,pronoun,%Ctx)),
verbs(kHA,%TRole1,%TRole2)
==>
in_context(%Ctx,role(%TRole1,kHA,%S),
in_context(%Ctx,role(%TRole2,kHA,%O).


context_head(%Ctx,%Pred),
uwn(%Pred,%Hyper)
==>
context_head(%Ctx,%Hyper).
```

Figure 8: Including lexical semantic information via XFR rules

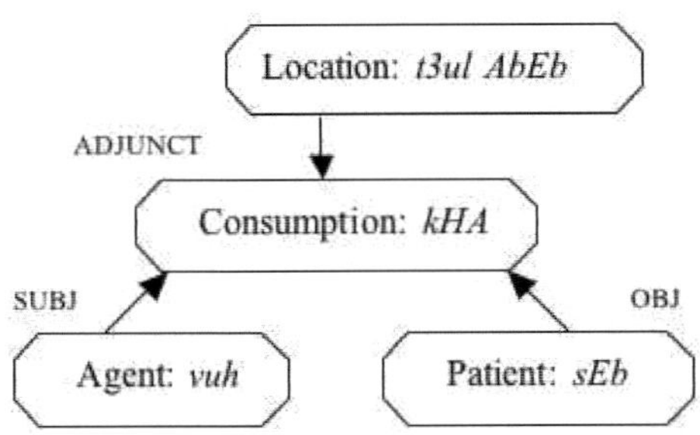

Figure 9: Final representation for *us nE t3ul AbEb meN sEb kHAyA* 'He ate an apple in Tel Aviv.'

4 Discussion

As for every computational grammar or semantic or analyzer, one wishes to have a thorough quantitative and qualitative evaluation justifying its robustness, coverage and accuracy, however we cannot provide such a justification in this paper. Although efforts are underway to create an independent gold standard for Urdu in the form of dependency triples as has been done for English (King et al., 2003), no such standard exists for Urdu to date. On the computational semantics side, this is also due to the fact that there has not been very much research in that direction.

The computational semantic analysis presented in this paper draws heavily on the syntactic analysis performed by the Urdu ParGram grammar. The more expressive the generated f-structures, the more detailed the semantic representations are. However, one could also use f-structures coming from other parsers whose output is reformatted according to the XLE standard and one could run the XFR system on these, potentially stochastic, f-structures as well.

As to adequate meaning representation, the overall move towards developing parallel semantics on top of parallel grammars within the ParGram community has only just started investigating appropriate representations of semantic concepts. The expressive power of a system also depends heavily on the external lexical resources that are available, in comparison to English, Urdu is far behind. However, with efforts like this computational semantic analyzer and the implementation of basic lexical resources we can contribute to the variety of tools available for Urdu.

5 Summary

In this paper we have presented a first approach to an automatic semantic analysis for Urdu, building on a deep and very detailed syntactic analysis by the Urdu ParGram Grammar. We have given a brief overview of the methodology of XFR rewrite rules, how they operate on top of LFG f-structures and what kind of semantic analysis they can provide. The inclusion of available lexical resources facilitates the generation of an abstract level of the representation of concepts rather than surface syntactic structure. We have also discussed some of the issues involved in building a semantic analyzer for a language where few other resources exist and where a lot of work has to go into the theoretical as well as the computationally efficient analysis of the language itself.

References

Tafseer Ahmed and Annette Hautli. 2010. An Experiment for a basic lexical resource for Urdu on the basis of Hindi WordNet. In *Proceedings of CLT 2010*, Islamabad, Pakistan.

Kenneth Beesley and Lauri Karttunen. 2003. *Finite State Morphology*. CSLI Publications, Stanford.

Rafiya Begum, Samar Husain, Lakshmi Bai, and Dipti Misra Sharma. 2008. Developing Verb Frames for Hindi. In *Proceedings of the Sixth International Language Resources and Evaluation (LREC'08)*, Marrakech, Morocco.

Pushpak Bhattacharyya, Prabhakar Pande, and Laxmi Lupu. 2008. *Hindi WordNet*. Linguistic Data Consortium, Philadelphia.

Pushpak Bhattacharyya. 2010. IndoWordNet. In *Proceedings of the Seventh conference on International Language Resources and Evaluation (LREC'10), Malta*.

Tina Bögel, Miriram Butt, Annette Hautli, and Sebastian Sulger. 2007. Developing a Finite-State Morphological Analyzer for Urdu and Hindi: Some Issues. In *Proceedings of FSMNLP07*. Postdam, Germany.

Tina Bögel, Miriram Butt, Annette Hautli, and Sebastian Sulger. 2009. Urdu and the Modular Architecture of ParGram. In *Proceedings of the Conference on Language and Technology (CLT09)*. CRULP, Lahore, Pakistan.

Johan Bos, Stephen Clark, Mark Steedman, James R. Curran, and Julia Hockenmaier. 2004. Wide-coverage semantic representations from a CCG parser. In *COLING '04: Proceedings of the 20th International Conference on Computational Linguistics*, page 1240.

Joan Bresnan and Ronald M. Kaplan, 1982. *The Mental Representation of Grammatical Relations*. The MIT Press, Cambridge.

Miriam Butt and Tracy Holloway King. 2002. Urdu and The Parallel Grammar Project. In *Proceedings of COLING2002, 3rd workshop on Asian language resources and international standardization*, pages 39–45, Taipei, Taiwan.

Miriam Butt, Tracy Holloway King, María-Eugenia Niño, and Frédérique Segond. 1999. *A Grammar Writer's Cookbook*. CSLI Publications, Stanford.

Miriam Butt, Helge Dyvik, Tracy Holloway King, Hiroshi Masuichi, and Christian Rohrer. 2002. The Parallel Grammar Project. In *Proceedings of COLING2002, Workshop on Grammar Engineering and Evaluation*, pages 1–7, Taipei, Taiwan.

Miriam Butt, Tina Bögel, and Sebastian Sulger. 2008. Urdu Ezafe and the Morphology-Syntax Interface. In Miriam Butt and Tracy Holloway King, editors, *Proceedings of LFG08*. CSLI Publications, Stanford.

Dick Crouch and Tracy Holloway King. 2006. Semantics via F-structure Rewriting. In *LFG06 Proceedings*. CSLI Publications, Stanford.

Dick Crouch, Mary Dalrymple, Ron Kaplan, Tracy King, John Maxwell, and Paula Newman. 2011. XLE Documentation. http://www2.parc.com/isl/groups/nltt/xle/doc/.

Mary Dalrymple, 2001. *Lexical Functional Grammar*, volume 34. Academic Press.

Christiane Fellbaum, editor. 1998. *WordNet: An Electronic Lexical Database*. Cambridge: The MIT Press.

Charles J. Fillmore. 1985. Frames and the Semantics of Understanding. *Quaderni di Semantica*, VI(2):222–254.

Annette Hautli and Sebastian Sulger. 2011. Extracting and Classifying Urdu Multiword Expressions. In *Proceedings of the 49th Annual Meeting of the Association for Computational Linguistics: Human Langauge Technologies (ACL-HLT '11): Student Session*, Portland, Oregon.

Tracy Holloway King, Richard Crouch, Stefan Riezler, Mary Dalrymple, and Ron Kaplan. 2003. The PARC700 Dependency Bank. In *Proceedings of the EACL03: 4th International Workshop on Linguistically Interpreted Corpora (LINC-03)*.

Karin Kipper-Schuler. 2005. *VerbNet: A Broad-Coverage, Comprehensive Verb Lexicon*. Ph.D. thesis, University of Pennsylvania.

Beth Levin. 1993. *English Verb Classes and Alternations*. Chicago: The University of Chicago Press.

Muhammad Kamran Malik, Tafseer Ahmed, Sebastian Sulger, Tina Bögel, Atif Gulzar, Ghulam Raza, Sarmad Hussain, and Miriam Butt. 2010. Transliterating Urdu for a Broad-Coverage Urdu/Hindi LFG Grammar. In *Proceedings of the Seventh conference on International Language Resources and Evaluation (LREC'10), Malta*.

Ghulam Raza and Tafseer Ahmed. 2011. Argument Scrambling within Urdu NPs. In *Proceedings of LFG11*, Hong Kong.

Stefan Riezler, Tracy Holloway King, Ronald M. Kaplan, Richard Crouch, John T. Maxwell, and Mark Johnson. 2002. Parsing the Wall Street Journal using a Lexical-Functional Grammar and Discriminative Estimation Techniques. In *Proceedings of the 40th Annual Meeting of the Association for Computational Linguistics (ACL'02)*, Philadephia, PA.

Josef van Genabith and Dick Crouch. 1996. Direct and underspecified interpretations of LFG f-structures. In *Proceedings of the 16th International Conference on Computational Linguistics (COLING-96)*, volume 1, pages 262–267, Copenhagen, Denmark.

Word Disambiguation in Shahmukhi to Gurmukhi Transliteration

Tejinder Singh Saini
ACTDPL, Punjabi University,
Patiala, Punjab-147 002, India
tej74i@gmail.com

Gurpreet Singh Lehal
DCS, Punjabi University,
Patiala, Punjab-147 002, India
gslehal@gmail.com

Abstract

To write Punjabi language, Punjabi speakers use two different scripts, Perso-Arabic (referred as Shahmukhi) and Gurmukhi. Shahmukhi is used by the people of Western Punjab in Pakistan, whereas Gurmukhi is used by most people of Eastern Punjab in India. The natural written text in Shahmukhi script has missing short vowels and other diacritical marks. Additionally, the presence of ambiguous character having multiple mappings in Gurmukhi script cause ambiguity at character as well as word level while transliterating Shahmukhi text into Gurmukhi script. In this paper we focus on the word level ambiguity problem. The ambiguous Shahmukhi word tokens have many interpretations in target Gurmukhi script. We have proposed two different algorithms for Shahmukhi word disambiguation. The first algorithm formulates this problem using a state sequence representation as a Hidden Markov Model (HMM). The second approach proposes n-gram model in which the joint occurrence of words within a small window of size ± 5 is used. After evaluation we found that both approaches have more than 92% word disambiguation accuracy.

1 Introduction

1.1 Shahmukhi Script

Shahmukhi is a derivation of the Perso-Arabic script used to record the Punjabi language in Pakistan. Shahmukhi script has thirty eight letters, including four long vowel signs Alif ا[ɘ], Vao و[v], Choti-ye ی[j] and Badi-ye ے[j]. Shahmukhi script in general has thirty seven simple consonants and eleven frequently used aspirated consonants. There are three nasal consonants (ݨ[ɳ], ن[n], م[m]) and one additional nasalization sign, called Noon-ghunna ں [ɲ].

In addition to this, there are three short vowel signs called Zer ◌ِ[ɪ], Pesh ◌ُ[ʊ] and Zabar ◌َ[ə] and some other diacritical marks or symbols like hamza ء[ɪ], Shad ◌ّ, Khari-Zabar ◌ٰ[ɘ], do-Zabar ◌ً[ən] and do-Zer ◌ٍ[ɪn] etc. Arabic orthography does not provide full vocalization of the text, and the reader is expected to infer short vowels from the context of the sentence. Any machine transliteration or text to speech synthesis system has to automatically guess and insert these missing symbols. This is a non-trivial problem and requires an in depth statistical analysis (Durrani and Hussain, 2010).

1.2 Gurmukhi Script

The Gurmukhi script, standardized by Guru Angad Dev in the 16th century, was designed to write the Punjabi language (Sekhon, 1996); (Singh, 1997). It was modeled on the *Landa* alphabet. The literal meaning of "Gurmukhi" is *from the mouth of the Guru*. The Gurmukhi script has syllabic alphabet in which all consonants have an inherent vowel. The Gurmukhi alphabet has forty one letters, comprising thirty eight consonants and three basic vowel sign bearers. The first three letters Ura ੳ[ʊ], Aira ਅ [ə] and Iri ੲ[ɪ] of Gurmukhi alphabet are unique because they form the basis for vowels and are not consonants. The six consonants are created by placing a *dot* at the foot (pair) of the existing consonant. There are five nasal consonants (ਙ[ɲə], ਞ[ɲə], ਣ[ɳ], ਨ[n], ਮ[m]) and two additional nasalization signs, bindi ◌ਂ [ɲ] and tippi ◌ੰ [ɲ] in Gurmukhi script. In addition to this, there are nine dependent vowel signs (or diacritics) (◌ੁ[ʊ], ◌ੂ [u], ◌ੋ[o], ◌ਾ[ɘ], ਿ◌[ɪ], ◌ੀ[i], ◌ੇ[e], ◌ੈ[æ], ◌ੌ[Ɔ]) used to create ten independent vowels (ੳ

Proceedings of the 9th Workshop on Asian Language Resources, pages 79–87,
Chiang Mai, Thailand, November 12 and 13, 2011.

[ʊ], ਊ [u], ਓ [o], ਅ [ə], ਆ [ɑ], ਇ [ɪ], ਈ [i], ਏ [e], ਐ [æ], ਔ [ɔ]) with three bearer characters: Ura ੳ[ʊ], Aira ਅ [ə] and Iri ੲ[ɪ]. With the exception of Aira ਅ [ə] independent vowels are never used without additional vowel signs. The diacritics which can appear above, below, before or after the consonant they belong to, are used to change the inherent vowel and when they appear at the beginning of a syllable, vowels are written as independent vowels. Some Punjabi words require consonants to be written in a conjunct form in which the second consonant is written under the first as a subscript. There are three commonly used subjoined consonants as shown here Haha ਹ[h] (usage ਨ[n] + ◌੍ + ਹ[h] = ਨ੍ਹ [n^h]), Rara ਰ[r] (usage ਪ[p] + ◌੍ + ਰ[r] =ਪ੍ਰ [pr^h]) and Vava ਵ[v] (usage ਸ[s] + ◌੍ + ਵ[v] = ਸ੍ਵ [sv]).

1.3 Transliteration and Ambiguity

To understand the problem of word ambiguity in the transliterated text let us consider a Shahmukhi sentence having total 13 words out of them five are ambiguous. During transliteration phase our system generates all possible interpretations in target script. Therefore, with this input the transliterated text has supplied all the ambiguous words with maximum two interpretations in the Gurmukhi script as shown in Figure 1.

اس دور وچ سبھ توں طاقتور اتے چلاک ویکتی قبیلے دا مکھی رہا

ਇਸ ਦੌਰ ਵਿਚ ਸਭ ਤੋਂ ਤਾਕਤਵਰ ਅਤੇ ਚਲਾਕ ਵਿਅਕਤੀ ਕਬੀਲੇ ਦਾ ਮੁਖੀ ਰਿਹਾ

is daur vic sabh tōṃ tākatvar atē calāk viaktī kabīlē dā mukhī rihā

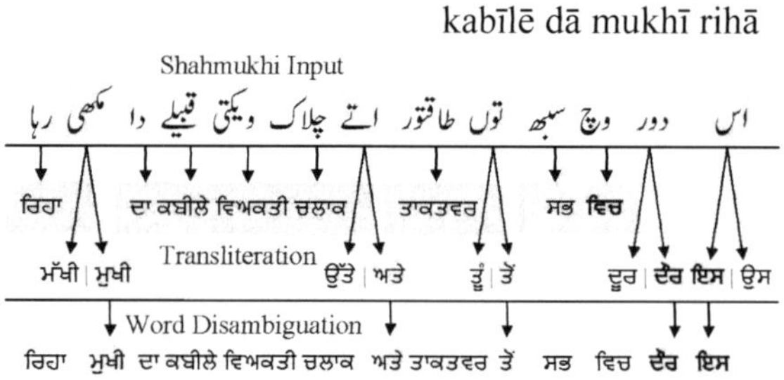

Figure 1. Word level Ambiguity in Transliterated Text

In a bigram statistical word disambiguation approach, the probability of co-occurrence of various alternatives such as <bos> ਇਸ |<bos> ਉਸ, ਇਸ ਦੌਰ | ਉਸ ਦੌਰ, ਇਸ ਦੂਰ | ਉਸ ਦੂਰ, ਦੌਰ ਵਿਚ | ਦੂਰ ਵਿਚ, ਸਭ ਤੋਂ | ਸਭ ਤੂੰ, ਤੋਂ ਤਾਕਤਵਰ | ਤੂੰ ਤਾਕਤਵਰ, ਤਾਕਤਵਰ ਅਤੇ | ਤਾਕਤਵਰ ਉੱਤੇ, ਅਤੇ ਚਲਾਕ | ਉੱਤੇ ਚਲਾਕ, ਦਾ ਮੁਖੀ | ਦਾ ਮੱਖੀ, and ਮੁਖੀ ਰਿਹਾ | ਮੱਖੀ ਰਿਹਾ are examined in the training corpus to estimate the likelihood. If the joint co-occurrence of following <bos> ਇਸ, ਇਸ ਦੌਰ, ਦੌਰ ਵਿਚ, ਸਭ ਤੋਂ, ਤੋਂ ਤਾਕਤਵਰ, ਤਾਕਤਵਰ ਅਤੇ, ਅਤੇ ਚਲਾਕ, ਦਾ ਮੁਖੀ, and ਮੁਖੀ ਰਿਹਾ bigram tokens are found to be more likely then the disambiguation will decide ਇਸ, ਦੌਰ, ਤੋਂ, ਅਤੇ and ਮੁਖੀ respectively as expected. Unfortunately, due to limited training data size or data sparseness it is quite probable that some of the alternative word interpretations are missing in the training corpus. In such cases additional information about word similarity like POS tagger and thesaurus may be helpful.

1.4 Causes of Ambiguity

The most common reasons for this ambiguity are missing short vowels and the presence of ambiguous character having multiple mappings in Gurmukhi script.

Sr	Word without diacritics	Possible Gurmukhi Transliteration
1	گل	ਗੱਲ /gall/, ਗਿੱਲ /gill/, ਗੁੱਲ /gull/, ਗੁਲ /gul/
2	تک	ਤਕ /tak/, ਤੱਕ /takk/, ਤੁਕ /tuk/
3	مکھی	ਮੱਖੀ/makkhī/, ਮੁਖੀ/mukhī/
4	ہن	ਹਨ /han/, ਹੁਣ /huṇ/
5	جتھے	ਜਿਥੇ /jithē/, ਜਥੇ /jathē/
6	دسدا	ਦਿਸਦਾ /disdā/, ਦੱਸਦਾ /dassdā/
7	اک	ਅੱਕ /akk/, ਇੱਕ /ikk/
8	جٹّ	ਜੱਟ/jaṭṭ/, ਜੁੱਟ /juṭṭ /
9	اس	ਉਸ /us/, ਇਸ /is/
10	اتے	ਅਤੇ /atē/, ਉੱਤੇ /uttē/

Table 1. Ambiguous Shahmukhi Words without Short Vowels

In the written Shahmukhi script, it is not mandatory to put short vowels, called Aerab, below or above the Shahmukhi character to clear its sound leading to potential ambiguous transliteration to Gurmukhi as shown in Table 1. In our findings, Shahmukhi corpus has just 1.66% coverage of short vowels ◌ُ[ʊ] (0.81415%),

ِ[ɪ](0.7295%), and ُ(0.1234%) whereas the equivalent ਿ[ɪ] (4.5462%) and ੁ[ʊ] (1.5844%) in Gurmukhi corpus has 6.13% usage. Hence, it is a big challenge in the process of machine transliteration process to recognize the right word from the written (without diacritic) text because in a situation like this, correct meaning of the word needs to be corroborated from its neighboring context.

Secondly, it is observed that there are multiple possible mappings in Gurmukhi script corresponding to a single character in the Shahmukhi script as shown in Table 2. Moreover, the shown characters of Shahmukhi have vowel-vowel, vowel-consonant and consonant-consonant mapping.

Sr	Char.	Multiple Gurmukhi Mappings
1	و [v]	ਵ [v], ੋ [o], ੌ [ɔ], ੁ [ʊ], ੂ [u], ਓ [o]
2	ی[j]	ਯ [j], ਿ [ɪ], ੇ [e], ੈ[æ], ੀ[i], ਈ [i]
3	ن[n]	ਨ [n], ੰ [ɲ], ਣ [ɳ], ਂ[ɲ]

Table 2. Multiple Mapping into Gurmukhi Script

For example, consider two Shahmukhi words چین /cīn/ and روس /rōs/ having the presence of an ambiguous character ی[i] and و[o] respectively. Our transliteration engine discovers the corresponding word interpretations as ਚੇਨ /cēn/, ਚੀਨ /cīn/, or ਚੈਨ /cain/ and ਰੋਸ /rōs/, or ਰੂਸ /rūs/ respectively. Furthermore, both the problems may coexist in a particular Shahmukhi word, for example, the Shahmukhi word بندی /baṇdī/ which has four different forms ਬਣਦੀ/baṇdī/, ਬੁਣਦੀ/buṇdī/, ਬੰਦੀ/bandī/ or ਬਿੰਦੀ/bindī/ in Gurmukhi script due to ambiguous character ن[n] and missing short vowel. More sample cases are shown in Table 3.

Another variety of word ambiguity mostly found in machine translation systems is where many words have several meanings or sense. The task of word sense disambiguation is to determine which of the sense of an ambiguous word is invoked in a particular use of the word. This is done by looking at the context of the ambiguous word and by exploiting contextual word similarities based on some predefined co-occurrence relations. The various types of disambiguation methods where the source of word similarity was either statistical (Schutze, 1992); (Dagan et al. 1993, 1995); (Karov and Shimon, 1996); (Lin, 1997); or using a manually crafted thesaurus (Resnik, 1992, 1995); (Jiang and Conrath, 1997); is presented in the literature.

Sr	Word with Ambiguous Char.		Possible Gurmukhi Transliteration
1	کھوہ	و [v]	ਖੂਹ / khūh/, ਖੋਹ /khōh/
2	پیو	ی[j]	ਪਿਓ /piō/, ਪੀਓ /pīō/
3	چین	ی[j]	ਚੇਨ /cēn/, ਚੀਨ /cīn/, ਚੈਨ /cain/
4	جاندا	ن[n]	ਜਾਂਦਾ /jāndā/, ਜਾਣਦਾ /jāṇdā/
5	سوچنا	و [v], ن[n]	ਸੂਚਨਾ /sūcnā/, ਸੋਚਣਾ /sōcaṇā/
6	دین	ی[j], ن[n]	ਦੇਣ /dēṇ/, ਦੀਨ /dīn/

Table 3. Shahmukhi Words with Multiple Gurmukhi Mappings

In this paper we have proposed two different algorithms for Shahmukhi word disambiguation. The first algorithm formulates this problem using a state sequence representation as a Hidden Markov Model (HMM). The second approach uses n-gram model in which the joint occurrence of words within a small window of size ± 5 is used.

2 The Level of Ambiguity in Shahmukhi Text

We have performed experiments to evaluate how much word level ambiguity is present in the Shahmukhi text. In order to measure the extent of such ambiguous words in a Shahmukhi corpus we have analyzed the top, most frequent 10,000 words obtained from the Shahmukhi word list that was generated during corpus analysis. The result of this analysis is shown in Table 4.

Sr.	Most Frequent Words	Percentage of Ambiguous words
1	Top 100	20%
2	Top 500	15.8%
3	Top 1,000	11.9%
4	Top 5,000	4.72%
5	Top 10,000	3.6%

Table 4. Extent of Ambiguity in Top 10K words of Shahmukhi Corpus

Observations:

- Most frequent words in Shahmukhi corpus have higher chances of being ambiguous.
- In this test case the maximum amount of ambiguity is 20% which is very high.

- The percentage of ambiguity decreases continuously while moving from most frequent to less frequent words within the list.
- The ambiguous words in Top 10,000 dataset have maximum four interpretations in Gurmukhi script with 2% coverage whereas the amount of three and two Gurmukhi interpretations is 12% and 86% respectively as shown in Figure 2.

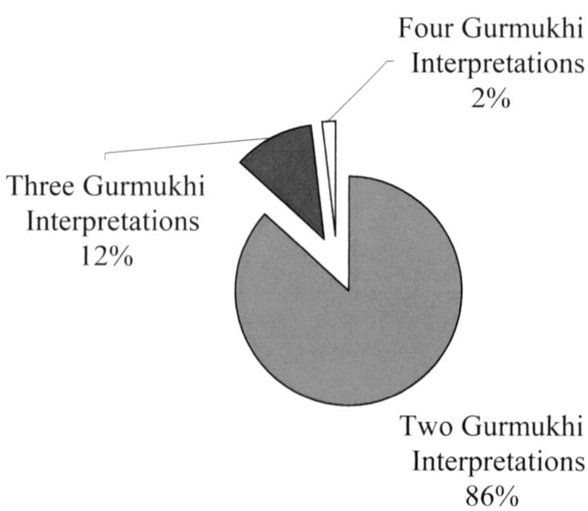

Figure 2. Number of Gurmukhi Interpretations of Ambiguous words in Top 10K Dataset

Additionally, a similar experiment was performed on a Shahmukhi book having a total of 37,620 words. After manual evaluation, we discovered that the extent of ambiguous words in this book was 17.12%. Hence, both the test cases figure out that there is significant percentage of ambiguous words in Shahmukhi text and must be addressed to achieve higher rate of transliteration accuracy.

3 The Approach

At the outset, all we have is the raw corpora for each (Shahmukhi and Gurmukhi) script of Punjabi language. The properties of these corpora are presented in Table 5. The majority of Shahmukhi soft data was found in the form of InPage software files. This soft data was converted to Unicode format using the InPage to Unicode Converter. A corpus based statistical analysis of both the corpora is performed. We have started from scratch and created the required resources in Unicode for both Shahmukhi and Gurmukhi scripts. The size of Gurmukhi training data used for word disambiguation task is shown in Table 6.

N-gram models are used extensively in language modeling and the same is proposed for Shahmukhi word disambiguation using the target script corpus. The N-grams have practical advantages to provide useful likelihood estimations for alternative reading of language corpora. Word similarities that are obtained from N-gram analysis are a combination of syntactical, semantic and contextual similarities those are very suitable in this task of word disambiguation.

Punjabi Script	Corpus Size	Unique words	Text Source
Gurmukhi	7.8 m	1,59,272	Daily and regional news papers, reports, periodicals, magazines, short stories and Punjabi literature books etc.
Shahmukhi	8.5 m	1,79,537	

Table 5. Properties of Shahmukhi and Gurmukhi Corpora

We have proposed two different algorithms for Shahmukhi word disambiguation. The first algorithm formulates this problem using a state sequence representation as a Hidden Markov Model. The second approach uses n-gram model (including the right side context) in which the joint occurrence of words within a small window of size ± 5 is used.

Training Data	Size (Records)
Gurmukhi Word Frequency List	87,962
Gurmukhi Bigram List	265,372
Gurmukhi Trigram List	247,010

Table 6. Training Data Resources

3.1 Word Disambiguation using HMM

Second order HMM is equivalent to n-gram language model with n=3 called trigram language model. One major problem with fixed n models is data sparseness. Therefore, one good idea to smooth n-gram estimates is to use linear interpolation (Jelinek and Mercer, 1980) of n-gram estimates for various n, for example:

$$P(w_n \mid w_{n-1}w_{n-2}) =$$
$$\lambda_1 P_1(w_n \mid w_{n-1}w_{n-2}) + \lambda_2 P_2(w_n \mid w_{n-1}) + \lambda_3 P_3(w_n)$$
$$\textit{where} \sum_i \lambda_i = 1 \text{ and } 0 \le \lambda_i \le 1 \qquad (2)$$

The variable n means that we are using trigram, bigram and unigram probabilities together as a linear interpolation. This way we would get some probability of how likely a particular word was, even if our coverage of trigram is sparse.

Now the next question is how to set the parameters λ_i. Thede and Harper, (1999) modeled a second order HMM for part of speech tagging. Rather than using fixed smoothing technique, they have discussed their new method of calculating contextual probabilities using the linear interpolation. This method attaches more weight to triples that occur more often. The formula to estimate contextual probability is:

$$P(\tau_p = w_k \mid \tau_{p-1} = w_j, \tau_{p-2} = w_i) =$$

$$k_3 . \frac{N_3}{C_2} + (1-k_3)k_2 . \frac{N_2}{C_1} + (1-k_3)(1-k_2) . \frac{N_1}{C_0}$$

where $k_3 = \frac{\log_2(N_3+1)+1}{\log_2(N_3+1)+2}$; and

$$k_2 = \frac{\log_2(N_2+1)+1}{\log_2(N_2+1)+2} \qquad (3)$$

The equation 2 depends on the following numbers:

N_3: Frequency of trigram $w_i w_j w_k$ in Gurmukhi corpus

N_2: Frequency of bigram $w_j w_k$ in Gurmukhi corpus

N_1: Frequency of unigram w_k in Gurmukhi corpus

C_2: Number of times bigram $w_i w_j$ occurs in Gurmukhi corpus

C_1: Number of times unigram w_j occurs in Gurmukhi corpus

C_0: Total number of words that appears in Gurmukhi corpus

The formulas for k_3 and k_2 are chosen so that the weighting for each element in the equation 2 for P changes based on how often that element occurs in the Gurmukhi corpus. After comparing the two equations 1 and 2, we can easily understand that:

$\lambda_1 = k_3$; $\lambda_2 = (1-k_3)k_2$; $\lambda_3 = (1-k_3)(1-k_2)$

and satisfy the condition $\sum_i \lambda_i = 1$; $0 \le \lambda_i \le 1$

We build an HMM with four states for each word pair, one for the basic word pair, and three representing each choice of n-gram model for calculating the next transition. Therefore, as expressed in equation 2 and 3 of second order HMM, there are three ways for w^c={ਦਸ or ਦੱਸ or ਦਿਸ} to follow $w^a w^b$ (ਹੁਣ ਤੂੰ) and the total probability of seeing w^c next is then the sum of each of the n-gram probabilities that adorn the arcs multiplied by the corresponding parameter $0 \le \lambda_i \le 1$. Correspondingly, the fragment of HMM for ambiguous Gurmukhi word sequence ਹੁਣ ਤੂੰ ਦੱਸ is shown in Figure 3 where the first two consecutive words have two forms {ਹਨ or ਹੁਣ} and {ਤੋਂ or ਤੂੰ} where as the third consecutive Gurmukhi word has three forms like {ਦਸ or ਦੱਸ or ਦਿਸ}.

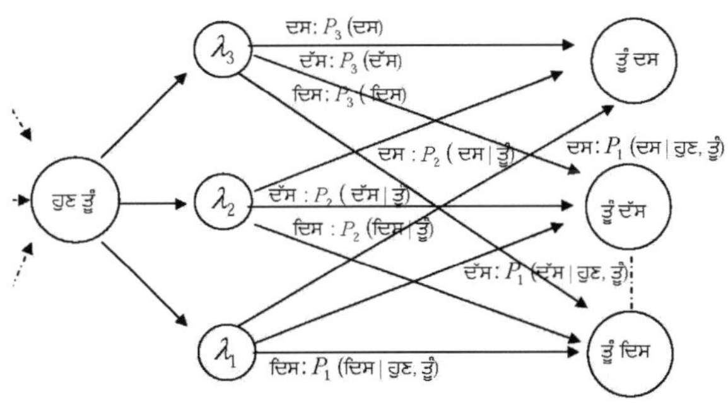

Figure 3. A Fragment of Second Order HMM for ਹੁਣ ਤੂੰ ਦੱਸ

To calculate the best state sequence we have modeled Viterbi Algorithm, which efficiently computes the most likely state sequence.

3.2 Word Disambiguation using ±5 Window Context

This n-gram based algorithm performs word disambiguation using the small window context of size ±5. This context is used to exploit the contextual, semantic and syntactical similarities based on the information captured by an n-gram language model. The structure of our small window context is shown in Figure 4.

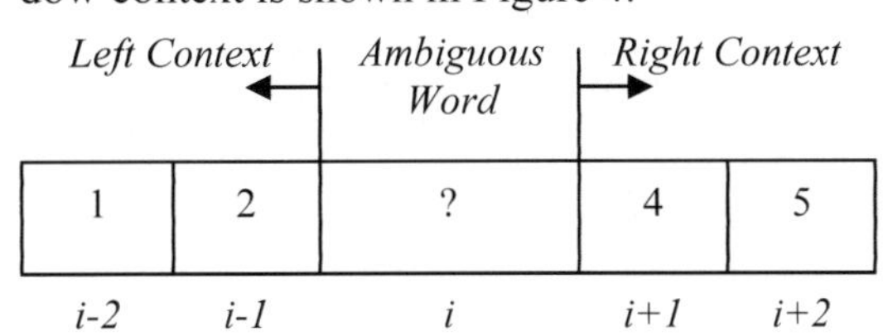

Figure 4. Structure of ±5 Window Context

The disambiguation task starts from the first word of the input sentence and attempts to investigate co-occurrence probabilities of the words present in the left and right of the ambiguous word within the window size. Unlike HMM approach which is based on linear interpolation of n-gram estimates (Jelinek and Mercer, 1980), this algorithm works in a back off fashion as proposed by Katz (1987) in which it first relies on highest order trigram model to estimate the joint co-occurrence possibility of alternative word interpretations to select the most probable interpretation. For example, consider the following Shahmukhi sentence with three ambiguous words as:

دس توں ہن

{ਦਸ ਦੱਸ ਦਿਸ} {ਤੋਂ ਤੂੰ} {ਹਨ ਹੁਣ}

The initial ambiguity is {ਹਨ /han/ | ਹੁਣ /huṇ/}, {ਤੋਂ /tōṃ/ | ਤੂੰ /tūṃ/} and {ਦਸ /das/ | ਦੱਸ /dass/ | ਦਿਸ /dis/}. The left and right context probabilities of the first ambiguous word are shown in Table 7.

<table>
<tr><th></th><th>Right Context</th><th></th><th>Left Context</th><th></th></tr>
<tr><th></th><th>Bigram</th><th>Trigram</th><th>Bigram</th><th>Trigram</th></tr>
<tr><td>ਹਨ</td><td>P(ਹਨ, ਤੋਂ |ਤੂੰ)</td><td>P(ਹਨ, ਤੋਂ |ਤੂੰ, ਦਸ | ਦੱਸ |ਦਿਸ)</td><td>P(_ , ਹਨ)</td><td>P(_ , _ , ਹਨ)</td></tr>
<tr><td>P=</td><td>0.000519</td><td>0.0</td><td>0.001613</td><td>0.001673</td></tr>
<tr><td>ਹੁਣ</td><td>P(ਹੁਣ, ਤੋਂ |ਤੂੰ)</td><td>P(ਹੁਣ, ਤੋਂ | ਤੂੰ, ਦਸ | ਦੱਸ |ਦਿਸ)</td><td>P(_ , ਹੁਣ)</td><td>P(_ , _ , ਹੁਣ)</td></tr>
<tr><td>P=</td><td>0.015945</td><td>0.037383</td><td>0.063967</td><td>0.064930</td></tr>
</table>

Table 7. Context Window Probabilities for ਹਨ and ਹੁਣ Words

Clearly, word ਹੁਣ is selected because it has higher trigram co-occurrence probability. Now the sentence ambiguity is reduced to ਹੁਣ {ਤੋਂ |ਤੂੰ} {ਦਸ | ਦੱਸ |ਦਿਸ}. The estimation of co-occurrence probability for next ambiguous word is shown in Table 8.

<table>
<tr><th></th><th>Right Context</th><th>Left Context</th><th></th></tr>
<tr><th></th><th>Bigram</th><th>Bigram</th><th>Trigram</th></tr>
<tr><td>ਤੋਂ</td><td>P(ਤੋਂ, ਦਸ |ਦੱਸ |ਦਿਸ)</td><td>P(ਹੁਣ, ਤੋਂ)</td><td>P(_ , ਹੁਣ, ਤੋਂ)</td></tr>
<tr><td></td><td>P=0.000492</td><td>P=0.006519</td><td>P=0.003341</td></tr>
<tr><td>ਤੂੰ</td><td>P(ਤੂੰ, ਦਸ |ਦੱਸ |ਦਿਸ)</td><td>P(ਹੁਣ, ਤੂੰ)</td><td>P(_ , ਹੁਣ, ਤੂੰ)</td></tr>
<tr><td></td><td>P=0.005019</td><td>P=0.009426</td><td>P=0.012454</td></tr>
</table>

Table 8. Context Window Probabilities for ਤੋਂ and ਤੂੰ Words

As expected, word ਤੂੰ is selected by the system using left trigram context and the sentence ambiguity is now reduced to ਹੁਣ ਤੂੰ {ਦਸ ਦੱਸ ਦਿਸ}. The next ambiguity is lying in the last word of the sentence so it has only left context as shown in Table 9. After evaluating the left context co-occurrence for all the three word forms the system found that the valid co-occurrence is P(ਹੁਣ, ਤੂੰ, ਦੱਸ) and on this basis word ਦੱਸ is selected. Finally, the output of the system is ਹੁਣ ਤੂੰ ਦੱਸ as expected.

	Right Context	Left Context	
		Bigram	**Trigram**
ਦਸ	N.A.	P(ਤੂੰ, ਦਸ)	P(ਹੁਣ, ਤੂੰ, ਦਸ)
	-	P=0020768	P=0
ਦੱਸ	N.A.	P(ਤੂੰ, ਦੱਸ)	P(ਹੁਣ, ਤੂੰ, ਦੱਸ)
	-	P=0.003980	**P=0.037383**
ਦਿਸ	N.A.	P(ਤੂੰ, ਦਿਸ)	P(ਹੁਣ, ਤੂੰ, ਦਿਸ)
	-	P=0.000028	P=0

Table 9. Context Window Probabilities for ਦਸ, ਦੱਸ and ਦਿਸ Words

Unlike the above example, there is a situation when the higher order joint co-occurrence is found to be zero in the training corpus. In this situation the proposed algorithm will back off to next lower n-1 gram model.

4 Example

Following is the N-gram and HMM outputs of word disambiguation task for the sample text downloaded from the article available on the web site *http://www.likhari.org*

Input Text

اسیں گلّ تاں کردے ہاں کہ اسیں اپنی ماں بولی نوں اسدا بندا حق دواؤن لئی پرزور ہاں پر ساڈیا اکھاں ساھمنے ہی پنجابی نال اسدے گھر وچ ہی نہ انصافی ہو رہی ہے تے اسیں چپّ چپّ کر کے ایہہ سبھ ویکھ رہے ہاں بھارت اتے پاکستان دوواں ملکاں ولوں پنجابی لئی ساںجھے منچ تے کم کیتا جا رہا ہے پچھلے دنیں بمبئی وچ جو کجھ واپریا اس نے ساری دنیاں نوں ہلا کے رکھ دتا اس نال دوواں ملکاں دے رشتے تڑکے ہن پر بدھیجیوی ورگ نوں اک گلّ اپنے ذہن وچ رکھنی چاہیدی ہے کہ سرحداں نے زمین ونڈی ہے زبان نہیں

Romanized:

asīṃ gall tāṃ karadē hāṃ ki asīṃ āpṇī māṃ bōlī nūṃ usdā baṇdā hakk divāuṇ laī purzōr hāṃ par sāḍīā akkhāṃ sāmhṇē hī pañjābī nāḷ usdē ghar vic hī nā iṃsāfī hō rahī hai tē asīṃ phir cupp kar kē ih sabh vēkh rahē hāṃ bhārat atē pākistān dōvāṃ mulkāṃ vallōṃ pañjābī laī sāñjhē mañc tē kamm kītā jā rihā hai pichlē dinīṃ bambī vic jō kujjh vāpriā us nē sārī dunīāṃ nūṃ hilā kē rakkh dittā is nāḷ dōvāṃ mulkāṃ dē rishtē taṛkē han par buddhījīvī varag nūṃ ikk gall āpaṇē zihan vic rakkhṇī cāhīdī hai ki sarhaddāṃ nē zamīn vaṇḍī hai zabān nahīṃ

N-gram Output:

ਅਸੀਂ **ਗੱਲ** ਤਾਂ ਕਰਦੇ ਹਾਂ ਕਿ ਅਸੀਂ ਆਪਣੀ ਮਾਂ ਬੋਲੀ **ਨੂੰ** ਉਸਦਾ **ਬਣਦਾ** ਹੱਕ ਦਿਵਾਉਣ ਲਈ ਪੁਰਜ਼ੋਰ ਹਾਂ **ਪਰ** **ਸਾਡਿਆ** ਅੱਖਾਂ ਸਾਮ੍ਹਣੇ ਹੀ ਪੰਜਾਬੀ ਨਾਲ਼ ਉਸਦੇ ਘਰ ਵਿਚ ਹੀ ਨਾ ਇੰਸਾਫ਼ੀ ਹੋ ਰਹੀ ਹੈ ਤੇ ਅਸੀਂ ਫਿਰ ਚੁੱਪ ਕਰ ਕੇ ਇਹ ਸਭ ਵੇਖ ਰਹੇ ਹਾਂ ਭਾਰਤ **ਅਤੇ** ਪਾਕਿਸਤਾਨ ਦੋਵਾਂ ਮੁਲਕਾਂ ਵੱਲੋਂ ਪੰਜਾਬੀ ਲਈ ਸਾਂਝੇ ਮੰਚ ਤੇ ਕੰਮ ਕੀਤਾ ਜਾ ਰਿਹਾ ਹੈ ਪਿਛਲੇ ਦਿਨੀਂ ਬੰਬਈ ਵਿਚ ਜੋ ਕੁੱਝ ਵਾਪਰਿਆ **ਉਸ** ਨੇ ਸਾਰੀ ਦੁਨੀਆਂ **ਨੂੰ** ਹਿਲਾ ਕੇ **ਰੱਖ** ਦਿੱਤਾ **ਇਸ** ਨਾਲ਼ ਦੋਵਾਂ ਮੁਲਕਾਂ ਦੇ ਰਿਸ਼ਤੇ ਤੜਕੇ **ਹਨ** **ਪਰ** ਬੁੱਧੀਜੀਵੀ ਵਰਗ **ਨੂੰ** **ਇਕ** **ਗੱਲ** ਆਪਣੇ ਜ਼ਿਹਨ ਵਿਚ ਰੱਖਣੀ ਚਾਹੀਦੀ ਹੈ ਕਿ ਸਰਹੱਦਾਂ ਨੇ ਜ਼ਮੀਨ ਵੰਡੀ ਹੈ ਜ਼ਬਾਨ ਨਹੀਂ

Ambiguous words (Total =15 i.e. 14.285%)

{ਗੱਲ ਗਿੱਲ ਗੁੱਲ ਗੁਲ}{ਨੂੰ ਨੈਂ}{ਬਣਦਾ ਬੰਦਾ}{ਪਰ ਪ੍ਰ ਪੁਰ}{ਸਾਡਿਆ ਸਾਡੀਆ}{ਅਤੇ ਉੱਤੇ}{ਉਸ ਇਸ}{ਨੂੰ ਨੈਂ}{ਰੱਖ ਰੁੱਖ}{ਇਸ ਉਸ ਐਸ}{ਹਨ ਹੁਣ}{ਪਰ ਪ੍ਰ ਪੁਰ}{ਨੂੰ ਨੈਂ}{ਇਕ ਅੱਕ ਇੱਕ}{ਗੱਲ ਗਿੱਲ ਗੁੱਲ ਗੁਲ}

2nd Order HMM Output:

ਅਸੀਂ **ਗੱਲ** ਤਾਂ ਕਰਦੇ ਹਾਂ ਕਿ ਅਸੀਂ ਆਪਣੀ ਮਾਂ ਬੋਲੀ **ਨੂੰ** ਉਸਦਾ **ਬਣਦਾ** ਹੱਕ ਦਿਵਾਉਣ ਲਈ ਪੁਰਜ਼ੋਰ ਹਾਂ **ਪਰ** **ਸਾਡੀਆ** ਅੱਖਾਂ ਸਾਮ੍ਹਣੇ ਹੀ ਪੰਜਾਬੀ ਨਾਲ਼ ਉਸਦੇ ਘਰ ਵਿਚ ਹੀ ਨਾ ਇੰਸਾਫ਼ੀ ਹੋ ਰਹੀ ਹੈ ਤੇ ਅਸੀਂ ਫਿਰ ਚੁੱਪ ਕਰ ਕੇ ਇਹ ਸਭ ਵੇਖ ਰਹੇ ਹਾਂ ਭਾਰਤ **ਅਤੇ** ਪਾਕਿਸਤਾਨ ਦੋਵਾਂ ਮੁਲਕਾਂ ਵੱਲੋਂ ਪੰਜਾਬੀ ਲਈ ਸਾਂਝੇ ਮੰਚ ਤੇ ਕੰਮ ਕੀਤਾ ਜਾ ਰਿਹਾ ਹੈ ਪਿਛਲੇ ਦਿਨੀਂ ਬੰਬਈ ਵਿਚ ਜੋ ਕੁੱਝ ਵਾਪਰਿਆ **ਉਸ** ਨੇ ਸਾਰੀ ਦੁਨੀਆਂ **ਨੂੰ** ਹਿਲਾ ਕੇ **ਰੱਖ** ਦਿੱਤਾ **ਇਸ** ਨਾਲ਼ ਦੋਵਾਂ ਮੁਲਕਾਂ ਦੇ ਰਿਸ਼ਤੇ ਤੜਕੇ **ਹਨ** **ਪਰ** ਬੁੱਧੀਜੀਵੀ ਵਰਗ **ਨੂੰ** **ਇੱਕ** **ਗੱਲ** ਆਪਣੇ ਜ਼ਿਹਨ ਵਿਚ ਰੱਖਣੀ ਚਾਹੀਦੀ ਹੈ ਕਿ ਸਰਹੱਦਾਂ ਨੇ ਜ਼ਮੀਨ ਵੰਡੀ ਹੈ ਜ਼ਬਾਨ ਨਹੀਂ

This sample input text has 105 words in total and around 14.28% ambiguity at word level. While processing, the disambiguation task identified that there are fifteen (bold face) words that are ambiguous, i.e. having two, three, and four interpretations in Gurmukhi script. The disambiguation results of this sample input show that out of fifteen ambiguous words fourteen have been correctly disambiguated by both the N-gram and HMM algorithms whereas only one wrong word ਸਾਡਿਆ /sāḍiā/ is mistakenly chosen by N-gram approach that has correctly recognized as ਸਾਡੀਆ /sāḍīā/ by the HMM algorithm.

5 Experiments and Results

The natural sources of Shahmukhi text are very limited. With this limitation we have identified the available online and offline sources and three different test sets are taken from different domains as shown in Table 10. After manual evaluation, the word disambiguation results on the three datasets are given in Table 11. The overall 13.85% word ambiguity corresponding to all datasets has a significant value. The upper bound contribution is from Set-1(book) having a highest percentage 17.12% of word ambiguity and the corresponding performance of two different disambiguation tasks is also highest.

Test Data	Word Size	Source
Set-1	37,620	*Book*
Set-2	39,714	*www.likhari.org*
Set-3	46678	*www.wichaar.com*
Total	**1,24,012**	

Table 10. Description of the Test Data

We have evaluated both HMM and N-gram algorithms on these datasets and the results of this experiment have shown that the accuracy of N-grams and HMM based algorithms is 92.81% and 93.77% respectively. Hence, the HMM based approach has outperformed marginally.

Test Data	Word Ambiguity	N-gram size ± 5	2nd order HMM
Set-1 (book)	17.121%	95.358%	95.870%
Set-2 (likhari.org)	12.587%	91.189%	91.629%
Set-3 (wichaar.com)	11.85%	91.892%	93.822%
Total	**13.85%**	**92.813%**	**93.773%**

Table 11. Word Disambiguation Result

The accuracy of both algorithms is more that 92%, indicating there is still room for improvement. A comparative analysis of both outputs is performed. We found that there are cases when both HMM and N-gram based methods individually outperform as shown in Table 12 row 1

& 2 and row 3 & 4 respectively. However, there are various cases in which both approaches fail to disambiguate either partially or fully as shown in row 5 & 6 of Table 12. It is observed that due to lack of training data both the proposed approaches have failed to distinguish correctly like ਅਤੇ /atē/ or ਉੱਤੇ /uttē/ as shown in 5th row of Table 12. Similarly, in some other cases system fails to predict name entity abbreviations as shown in 6th row of Table 12.

We can produce better results in the future by increasing the size of the training corpus and by exploiting contextual word similarities based on some predefined co-occurrence relations.

Sr.	N-gram Output	Word Ambiguity Correct = ✓	2nd order HMM Output
1	ਕਈ ਵਾਰ ਲੋਕਾਂ ਵਿਚੋਂ ਕੁੱਝ ਲੋਕ ਵੀ **ਇਕ** ਕੇ ਜ਼ੁਲਮ ਦਾ ਟਾਕਰਾ ਕਰਨ ਲਈ ਹਥਿਆਰ ਚੱਕ ਲੈਂਦੇ ਹਨ ਪਰ ਸੇਧ ਅਤੇ ਅਨੁਸ਼ਾਸਨ ਦੀ ਘਾਟ ਕਾਰਨ ਅਪਣਾ ਹੀ ਨੁਕਸਾਨ ਕਰਵਾ ਬੈਠਦੇ ਹਨ kaī vār lōkāṃ vicōṃ kujjh lōk vī ik kē zulam dā ṭākrā karan laī hathiār cakk laindē han par sēdh atē anushāsan dī ghāṭ kāran apṇā hī nuksān karavā baiṭhdē han	{ਇਕ **ਅੱਕ** ✓ ਇੱਕ}{ਹਨ ਹੁਣ}{ਪਰ ਪ੍ਰ ਪੁਰ}{ਅਤੇ ਉੱਤੇ}{ ਹਨ ਹੁਣ} {ik akk ikk}{han huṇ}{par pr pur}{atē uttē}{han huṇ}	ਕਈ ਵਾਰ ਲੋਕਾਂ ਵਿਚੋਂ ਕੁੱਝ ਲੋਕ ਵੀ **ਅੱਕ** ਕੇ ਜ਼ੁਲਮ ਦਾ ਟਾਕਰਾ ਕਰਨ ਲਈ ਹਥਿਆਰ ਚੱਕ ਲੈਂਦੇ ਹਨ ਪਰ ਸੇਧ ਅਤੇ ਅਨੁਸ਼ਾਸਨ ਦੀ ਘਾਟ ਕਾਰਨ ਅਪਣਾ ਹੀ ਨੁਕਸਾਨ ਕਰਵਾ ਬੈਠਦੇ ਹਨ kaī vār lōkāṃ vicōṃ kujjh lōk vī akk kē zulam dā ṭākrā karan laī hathiār cakk laindē han par sēdh atē anushāsan dī ghāṭ kāran apṇā hī nuksān karavā baiṭhdē han
2	ਆਪਣੇ ਘਰਦਿਆਂ **ਤੂੰ** ਵਿਆਹ ਦੀ ਆਸ ਲਾਹ ਛੱਡ āpaṇē ghardiāṃ tūṃ viāh dī ās lāh chaḍḍ	{ਤੂੰ **ਤੋਂ**✓ } {tūṃ tōṃ}	ਆਪਣੇ ਘਰਦਿਆਂ **ਤੋਂ** ਵਿਆਹ ਦੀ ਆਸ ਲਾਹ ਛੱਡ āpaṇē ghardiāṃ tōṃ viāh dī ās lāh chaḍḍ
3	ਬਚਪਨ ਵਿਚ ਅਸੀਂ ਉਨ੍ਹਾਂ ਕੋਲ਼ **ਜਾਂਦੇ** ਹੁੰਦੇ ਸੀ bacpan vic asīṃ unhāṃ kōḷ jāndē hundē sī	{**ਜਾਂਦੇ** ✓ ਜਾਣਦੇ} {jāndē jāṇdē}	ਬਚਪਨ ਵਿਚ ਅਸੀਂ ਉਨ੍ਹਾਂ ਕੋਲ਼ **ਜਾਣਦੇ** ਹੁੰਦੇ ਸੀ bacpan vic asīṃ unhāṃ kōḷ jāṇdē hundē sī
4	ਸਾਨੂੰ ਪੁੱਤਾਂ ਤੋਂ ਸਪਤ ਬਣਨ ਲਈ ਜੀਵਨ ਸੇਧ ਗੁਰੂ ਗ੍ਰੰਥ ਸਾਹਿਬ ਦੇ ਵਿਚ ਦਰਜ ਬਾਣੀ **ਤੋਂ** ਹੀ ਮਿਲ ਸਕਦੀ ਹੈ sānūṃ puttāṃ tōṃ sapat baṇan laī jīvan sēdh gurū granth sāhib dē vic daraj bāṇī tōṃ hī mil sakadī hai	{ਤੋਂ ਤੂੰ}{**ਤੋਂ** ✓ ਤੂੰ}{ਮਿਲ ਮੱਲ ਮਿੱਲ ਮੁੱਲ} {tōṃ tūṃ}{tōṃ tūṃ}{mil mall mill mull}	ਸਾਨੂੰ ਪੁੱਤਾਂ ਤੋਂ ਸਪਤ ਬਣਨ ਲਈ ਜੀਵਨ ਸੇਧ ਗੁਰੂ ਗ੍ਰੰਥ ਸਾਹਿਬ ਦੇ ਵਿਚ ਦਰਜ ਬਾਣੀ **ਤੂੰ** ਹੀ ਮਿਲ ਸਕਦੀ ਹੈ sānūṃ puttāṃ tōṃ sapat baṇan laī jīvan sēdh gurū granth sāhib dē vic daraj bāṇī tūṃ hī mil sakadī hai
5	ਮੇਰੇ **ਉੱਤੇ** ਅਨੁਪ੍ਰੀਤ ਦੇ ਹੈਮਿਲਟਨ ਰਹਿਣ ਕਰ ਕੇ ਜਸਜੀਤ ਵੀ ਸਾਡੇ ਪਾਸ ਆ ਗਈ mērē uttē anuprīt dē haimilṭan rahiṇ kar kē jasjīt vī sāḍē pās ā gaī	{ **ਅਤੇ**✓ ਉੱਤੇ} {atē uttē}	ਮੇਰੇ **ਉੱਤੇ** ਅਨੁਪ੍ਰੀਤ ਦੇ ਹੈਮਿਲਟਨ ਰਹਿਣ ਕਰ ਕੇ ਜਸਜੀਤ ਵੀ ਸਾਡੇ ਪਾਸ ਆ ਗਈ mērē uttē anuprīt dē haimilṭan rahiṇ kar kē jasjīt vī sāḍē pās ā gaī
6	ਪ੍ਰੋਫ਼ੈਸਰ **ਏਸ** ਐਨ ਮਿਸ਼ਰਾ prōfaisar ēs ain mishrā	{ਏਸ ਇਸ **ਐਸ**✓ } {ਐਨ ਇਨ} {ēs is ais} {ain in}	ਪ੍ਰੋਫ਼ੈਸਰ **ਇਸ** ਐਨ ਮਿਸ਼ਰਾ prōfaisar is ain mishrā

Table 12. Sample Failure Cases

References

Dekang Lin. 1997. Using syntactic dependency as local context to resolve word sense ambiguity. In *Proceedings of 35th Annual Meeting of the ACL and 8th Conference of the European Chapter of the Association for Computational Linguistics*. Madrid, Spain, 64-71.

Frederick Jelinek and Robert L. Mercer. 1980. Interpolated estimation of Markov source parameters from sparse data. In *Proceedings of the Workshop on Pattern Recognition in Practice*. Amsterdam, The Netherlands: North-Holland.

Harbhajan Singh. 1997. *Medieval Indian Literature: An Anthology*. Paniker K. Ayyappa, (Ed.) Sahitya Akademi Publication, volume 2, 417-452.

Hinrich Schütze. 1992. Dimensions of meaning. In *Proceedings of Supercomputing '92*. Minneapolis, MN, 787-796.

Ido Dagan, Shaul Marcus and Shaul Markovitch. 1993. Contextual word similarity and estimation from sparse data. In *Proceedings of the 31st annual meeting on Association for Computational Linguistics (ACL '93)*. Association for Computational Linguistics, Stroudsburg, PA, USA, 164-171. doi=10.3115/981574.981596

Ido Dagan, Shaul Marcus and Shaul Markovitch. 1995. Contextual word similarity and estimation from sparse data. *Computer Speech and Language*, 9:123-152.

Jay J. Jiang. David W. Conrath. 1997. Semantic similarity based on corpus statistics and lexical taxonomy. In *Proceedings of International Conference Research on Computational Linguistics (ROCLING)*. Taiwan, 1-15.

Lawrence R. Rabiner. 1989. A Tutorial on Hidden Markov Models and Selected Applications in Speech Recognition. *Proceedings of the IEEE*, 77(2):257-285.

Nadir Durrani and Sarmad Hussain. 2010. Urdu word segmentation. *Human Language Technologies: The 2010 Annual Conference of the North American Chapter of the Association for Computational Linguistics*, Los Angeles, California, 528-536.

Philip Resnik. 1992. WordNet and distributional analysis: A class-based approach to lexical discovery. In *Proceedings of AAAI Workshop on Statistically-based Natural Language Processing Techniques*. Menlo Park, California, 56-64.

Philip Resnik. 1995. Disambiguating noun groupings with respect to WordNet senses. In *Proceedings of the Third Workshop on Very Large Corpora*. Cambridge, 54-68

Ralph Grishman and John Sterling. 1993. Smoothing of automatically generated selectional constraints. In *Proceedings of DARPA Conference on Human Language Technology*. San Francisco, California, 254-259.

Ralph Grishman, Lynette Hirschman and Ngo Thanh Nhan. 1986. Discovery procedures for sublanguage selectional patterns: initial experiments. *Computational Linguistics*, 12(3):205-215.

Sant S. Sekhon. 1996. *A History of Panjabi Literature*, Publication Bureau, Punjabi University, Patiala, volume 1 & 2, Punjab, India.

Scott M. Thede and Mary P. Harper. 1999. A second-order Hidden Markov Model for part-of-speech tagging. In *Proceedings of the 37th annual meeting of the Association for Computational Linguistics on Computational Linguistics (ACL '99)*. Association for Computational Linguistics, Stroudsburg, PA, USA, 175-182. doi=10.3115/1034678.1034712

Slava M. Katz. 1987. Estimation of probabilities from sparse data for the language model component of a speech recognizer. *IEEE Transactions on Acoustics, Speech and Signal Processing*, ASSP, 35(3):400-401.

Ute Essen and Volker Steinbiss. 1992. Cooccurrence smoothing for stochastic language modeling. In *Proceedings of the 1992 IEEE international conference on Acoustics, speech and signal processing - Volume 1 (ICASSP'92)*, IEEE Computer Society, Washington, DC, USA, 161-164.

Yael Karov and Shimon Edelman. 1996. Learning similarity-based word sense disambiguation from sparse data. In *Proceedings of the Fourth Workshop on Very Large Corpora*. Copenhagen, Denmark, 42-55.

Author Index

Association for Computational Linguistics
209 N. Eighth Street
Stroudsburg, Pennsylvania 18360